AP® World History EXPRESS

KAPLAN) PUBLISHING
New York

AP® is a registered trademark of the College Board, which neither sponsors nor endorses this product.

© 2010 by Kaplan, Inc.

Published by Kaplan Publishing, a division of Kaplan, Inc.
395 Hudson Street
New York, NY 10014

Printed in the United States of America

10 9 8 7 6 5 4 3 2 1

ISBN 978-1-60714-787-9

Kaplan Publishing books are available at special quantity discounts to use for sales promotions, employee premiums, or educational purposes. For more information or to purchase books, please call the Simon & Schuster special sales department at 866-506-1949

Table of Contents

How to Take the Test

❯❯ ABOUT THIS BOOK

If you are taking an AP World History course at your high school, or if you have a good foundation in historical analysis and strong composition skills, taking the exam can help you earn college credit and placement into advanced coursework. Think of the money and time you can save! It can also improve your chances of acceptance to competitive schools, because colleges know that AP students are better prepared for college.

In the following pages, you will find information about the format of the exam, test-taking strategies, and an extensive review of essential topics that will help you to identify your strengths and weaknesses, and establish a study plan.

The first thing you need to do is find out what is on the AP World History exam. The next section of this introduction presents the overall test structure and a brief overview of its scoring. You'll find background information about the test and the most effective test strategies to help you score your best, including guidelines for successful multiple-choice testing and essay construction.

> ❯ **AP EXPERT TIP**
>
> Try to allow yourself at least 30 minutes nightly to review. Use this guide, along with your textbook, class handouts, and Internet resources for content mastery.

❯❯ ABOUT THE TEST

The AP World History exam is 3 hours and 5 minutes long. You will have 55 minutes to complete the first section, which consists of 70 multiple-choice questions. You will have 2 hours and 10 minutes to complete the second section, which consists of 3 essay questions.

Section I: Multiple-choice	70 questions	55 minutes	50% of the exam
Section II: Essays	3 questions	130 minutes	50% of the exam

Almost all parts of the world are covered on the AP World History exam, although some areas are covered more extensively than others. The majority of the questions on the World History exam are about places outside of Europe, such as Asia, Africa, and Latin America. European history accounts for at most 30 percent of the exam. U.S. history is not emphasized, except when it involves relationships with other areas of the world and larger global issues.

Time Period and Weight on the Exam	
To c. 600 BCE	5%
c. 600 BCE to c. 600 CE	15%
c. 600 CE to c. 1450	20%
c. 1450 to c. 1750	20%
c. 1750 to c. 1900	20%
c. 1900 to the present	20%

The test covers approximately 8000 BCE to the present. However, there is a gap between when the test is created and when it is administered. You do *not* need to know current events or the very recent past.

In addition to the major time periods, the AP curriculum is structured around five broad historical themes. Being familiar with these themes will help you on both sections of the test. Each theme is broken down into key topics. Knowing these will help you focus your study.

Theme 1: Interaction Between Humans and the Environment

- Demography and disease
- Migration
- Patterns of settlement
- Technology

Theme 2: Development and Interaction of Cultures

- Religions
- Belief systems, philosophies, and ideologies
- Science and technology
- The arts and architecture

Theme 3: State Building, Expansion, and Conflict

- Political structures and forms of governance
- Empires
- Nations and nationalism
- Revolts and revolutions
- Regional, transregional, and global structures and organizations

Theme 4: Creation, Expansion, and Interaction of Economic Systems

- Agricultural and pastoral production
- Trade and commerce
- Labor systems
- Industrialization
- Capitalism and socialism

Theme 5: Development and Transformation of Social Structures

- Gender roles and relations
- Family and kinship
- Racial and ethnic constructions
- Social and economic classes

For more information about the AP World History exam and other AP exams, check the College Board AP website at **apcentral.collegeboard.com**.

❯❯ WHAT THE TEST REQUIRES

Although the AP World History exam is not a test that one passes or fails, generally a 3 or higher on the 5-point scale is necessary to receive advanced placement, credit, or both from the college of your choice.

The best way to find out what the test requires is to look at the practice sections in this book. They include detailed explanations of the answers to each question. There are sample student responses for each essay question. Use the scoring guides provided to get a sense of your own strengths and weaknesses.

The AP World History exam tests your critical and analytical thinking skills and your knowledge of major time periods and trends. The multiple-choice and essay questions require you to apply key historical issues and themes. However, the exam does not test your knowledge of specific dates. You will also be asked to observe textual details, make comparisons, establish connections, and draw meaningful conclusions.

❯❯ HOW THE TEST IS SCORED

The multiple-choice section makes up half of your score. Your score for the multiple-choice section is based on the total number of correct answers. **No points are deducted for wrong answers.** The essay section makes up the other half of your score. Your essays are read and graded by trained AP teachers and college faculty. These two scores are combined to give a composite score, which is converted to the AP's 5-point scale. All AP exams are rated on a scale of 1 to 5, with 5 as the highest:

5 Extremely well qualified

4 Well qualified

3 Qualified

2 Possibly qualified

1 No recommendation

> **❯ AP EXPERT TIP**
>
> Many states post online or offer in hard copy the AP test score requirements for the various colleges and universities within the state. These will vary from state to state, just as score requirements vary from college to college.

❯❯ HOW TO APPROACH THE MULTIPLE-CHOICE SECTION

The multiple-choice questions cover all time periods, from prehistory to the present, and are arranged in chronological groups. In addition, some questions will ask about a single country, region, or topic across chronological boundaries. For example, you might be asked about the fundamental tenets of a religion. Questions are often comparative both within and across time frames. Although there is no firm rule for the organization of content, the test typically cycles through all of the time periods at least twice.

Here are some tips for doing well on the multiple-choice section of the test:

Answer in Your Own Order

The questions do not appear in order of difficulty. The last question could be the easiest, so you want to make sure you get through all of the questions. Rather than taking the test in a completely linear way, use these steps:

1. Answer all the questions that you know and are sure about first.

2. Go through the questions you were not sure about and mark them based on your familiarity with the topic.
   - If the topic is familiar and you can eliminate at least two answer choices, mark the question by **circling** the question number, and move on.
   - If you do *not* remember the topic, mark the question with an **X**, and move on.

3. Go back through the test and answer the questions circled. Try to eliminate at least three choices, then take your best guess.

4. Go back and answer the questions you marked with an X. Again, try to eliminate at least two or three choices, and take an educated guess.

Read Actively

The main part of a test question, before the answer choices, is called the *stem*. Read the question stem carefully, paying particular attention to key words such as *only*, *except*, *always*, *not*, *never*, and *best*. Underline key words and phrases in the question.

Predict an Answer

Before you look at the answer choices, try to think of the answer on your own. This will help you narrow the choices and avoid being seduced by wrong answers that *seem* right at first glance. Wrong answer choices are also known as *distracters* because they *distract* you from the right answer.

Use the Process of Elimination

As you read through the possible responses, cross off the ones you know are wrong. Be sure to read every possible answer before you make your selection. When eliminating distracters think about whether each choice is outside of the time period, region, or category of the question.

Pace Yourself

You have 55 minutes to complete 70 questions. Move quickly but thoroughly through the test. Do not linger on any single question for more than about 30 seconds.

If you have time remaining after you have completed all of the questions, go back and check your answers and check to make sure you have gridded in all responses correctly.

Remember, every correct answer adds to your score, and there is no penalty for incorrect answers. **So be sure to answer every question!**

Practice multiple-choice questions, with detailed answer explanations, are provided at the ends of chapters 1 and 5.

❯❯ HOW TO APPROACH THE ESSAY QUESTIONS

The second part of the AP World History exam is the essay section. This section inspires the most dread in the minds of students taking the test. However, understanding the structure, timing, and scoring of the essays can give you a big advantage.

Part A, the document-based question (DBQ), asks you to analyze information based on several historical documents provided. A sample DBQ question is provided at the end of Chapter 2.

Part B, continuity and change over time (CCOT) asks you to show your knowledge of a topic across time periods. A sample CCOT question is provided at the end of Chapter 3.

Part C, the comparative question (COMP), asks you to focus on broad historical issues and at least two societies. A sample COMP question is provided at the end of Chapter 4.

Here are some tips for doing well on the essay section of the test:

Answer in Your Own Order

You do not have to answer the essays in the order in which they appear. When you open your essay test packet, scan the three questions and choose the essay for which you have the most ready response. Beginning with your strongest area will help boost your confidence.

Read Critically

Before you begin writing, read and decode the essay prompt carefully. What is it asking? Is there more than one part to the question? Read the prompt with your pen in your hand. Underline, circle, and make notations.

Organize and Structure Your Essay

For each type of essay question, be sure to:

- have a relevant thesis or position
- support that thesis with historical evidence
- address all parts of the question
- analyze and explain—don't summarize

> ▶ **AP EXPERT TIP**
>
> You will have to use black or blue ink to write your essays. If you are used to writing in pencil or typing, practice writing in ballpoint pen. Use a comfortable pen that has a finger cushion and a wider diameter.

Don't include personal opinions in the essay. The reader is looking for your grasp of the history itself and your ability to write about it.

Stick to the topic and time period. Giving historical information before or after the period of the essay will not win you any points.

A longer essay is not necessarily better, but it takes more than a paragraph or two to merit a good score. As a general rule, aim for five parts: an introduction, three body paragraphs, and a conclusion. Another good rule of thumb is one body paragraph for each portion of the essay prompt.

Write It Out

Write as neatly and as legibly as you can. Test scorers understand that your essays are drafts. Cross-outs, inserted lines with arrows, and other working thoughts are acceptable as long as they are clear. However, avoid using abbreviations, shorthand symbols (such as & or @) or texting spelling. If the reader does not understand the symbol or word, he or she will ignore it, and you might not gain a point.

You must write an *essay* for each question. Bulleted notes, diagrams, or lists of information are not considered essay format and will be ignored by the reader.

Pace Yourself

A total of 130 minutes, or 2 hours and 10 minutes, is allotted for reading, organizing, and writing all three questions. The first 10 minutes are a mandatory reading period. Your proctor will *not* tell you to move from one essay to the next—you must do this on your own.

Essay Type	Budgeted Time
DBQ	50 min. (includes 10 min. reading period)
CCOT	40 min.
COMP	40 min.

Each essay counts the same amount in your final score. You do not want to rush through the essays too quickly, and you especially do not want to run out of time. Partial essays do not receive high scores. Bring a watch, and budget your time for each essay.

Practice essay questions, with scoring guides and strategies for each of the three question types, are provided at the ends of chapters 2, 3, and 4.

▶ AP EXPERT TIPS

1. Remember the strategies of Pacing, Process of Elimination, and Reading Critically.
2. Know how to manage your stress. You can beat anxiety the same way you can beat the exam—by knowing what to expect beforehand and developing strategies to deal with it.
3. Take Kaplan's practice tests to learn your test-taking strengths and weaknesses. Knowing these will allow you to focus on your problem areas as you prepare for test day.
4. Get organized! Make a study schedule between now and test day and give yourself plenty of time to prepare. Waiting until the last minute to cram info is not only unwise but exhausting.
5. Make a test day game plan. Have everything you need to bring to the exam ready the night before. Make it a priority to eat a good breakfast. Avoid overindulging in caffeine. Read something to warm up your brain. And finally, get to the test site early.

CHAPTER 1

Beginnings (8000 BCE to 600 CE)

⟫ A THUMBNAIL VIEW

- From the simplest barter system to long journeys along trade routes, the exchange of goods and ideas shaped this period and led to further change throughout the world. Important trade routes like the Silk Roads, Indian Ocean, and Mediterranean Sea influenced development.

> ⟫ AP EXPERT TIP

As we look at more specific information in this review, be aware of the theme the information is addressing. Also note changes and continuities and why the change or continuity occurred.

- Once people began to settle and gradually organize into early civilizations, the development of agriculture began to change their lives at a more rapid pace. In terms of farming, the Neolithic Revolution was a world-altering event. Alternatively, people living in the Eurasian Steppe developed pastoral nomadism. Also, the use of metals flourished; from the development of copper, bronze, and then iron, the use of metallurgy allowed humans to develop stronger and more efficient weapons and tools.

- As humans organized themselves in families, gender roles emerged. With the development of agriculture, the division of labor further deepened these divisions. These gender roles were reinforced by religious systems and governmental systems. In almost all cultures outside of Africa, women were excluded from positions of power, a condition known as patriarchy. In most cultures, women had some protective rights, but in others, patriarchal societies emerged. This patriarchy was often reinforced by organized religion.

- During this period, major world religions developed and spread, shaping the civilizations they encountered. Religions and belief systems such as Hinduism, Buddhism, Confucianism, and Daoism (Asia) and Christianity and Judaism (Europe, Asia) influenced large numbers of people throughout the period.

- Civilizations emerged that had organized governments, complex religions, social structures, job specialization, public works, systems of writing, and arts and architecture. These civilizations grew into larger and more complicated governmental organizations such as empires (e.g., Rome, Han, and Gupta). The accumulation of a food surplus allowed some members of society to do things other than farm. This led to job specialization and the beginnings of social class structures based on economic roles: for example, aristocrats (nobles), artisans (craftsmen or tradesmen), and peasants.

- As civilizations developed, so did the need to keep records and further communicate systems of writing. Around the world, people expressed themselves through the arts, from the earliest cave paintings to great works of architecture.

❯❯ NEOLITHIC REVOLUTION

Early humans lived for thousands of years hunting animals and gathering roots and plants. Around 8000 BCE, a dramatic breakthrough in human history called the **Neolithic Revolution** changed the way people lived. It might have been called the Neolithic *transition*, though, since it took hundreds, if not thousands, of years of change before an agricultural economy took hold.

Time and World Population	
10000 BCE	4 million
5000 BCE	5 million
3000 BCE	14 million
2000 BCE	27 million
1000 BCE	50 million
500 BCE	100 million

The development of agriculture, most likely begun by women who were experimenting with seeds they had gathered, allowed people to change the way they lived. The first farmers used **slash-and-burn agriculture,** in which they would slash the bark of trees and burn them to the ground. The problem was that although the land was initially very fertile, it lost much of that fertility after a few years. This caused people to migrate to new areas, helping to facilitate the spread of agriculture to new areas. A second great discovery was the **breeding of animals.** With these tools, people could now remain in one place for several years rather than moving constantly.

While farming was a lot more work (the average hunter and gatherer worked only four hours a day to find food), it was also a lot more stable. Hunters and gatherers had very small families, but now that people had stopped moving as much, families grew.

Life in a Neolithic Village

Early farmers began to organize themselves in a more permanent way through the formation of villages. This permanence allowed for the development of new technologies (farming tools such as the hoe, for instance). Farmers began to produce a **surplus** of food, and once a surplus was produced, **job specialization** was allowed to develop. Other jobs such as metalsmith, miller, brewer, trader, and priest provided services for the farmers—and the farmers could provide them food.

The private ownership of land equaled economic power. Land was kept in families' hands and passed down from generation to generation; with this, social class emerged. It was the new wealthiest class who desired luxury items, which could be traded with other communities.

For the Neolithic people, nature meant life or death. They had to learn the changes of the seasons based on the position of the sun, moon, and stars. Religiously, their main goal was to ensure fertility—both theirs and the land's. Religious beliefs centered on the life cycle of birth, growth, death, and regenerated life. Clay figurines of gods and goddesses that reflect this belief have been unearthed.

The Neolithic Revolution also had consequences for **gender roles.** Men were working in the fields and herding the animals, which required them to be outside the home. On the other hand, women performed such jobs as caring for the children, weaving cloth, and making cheese from milk, all of which required them to be in the home. Over time, the work outside the home was perceived as more important, and men began to take a more dominant role in the gender relationship.

Early Inventions in Metal and Transportation

In Neolithic villages, three main craft industries developed and became essential elements of almost all human agricultural societies: pottery, metallurgy, and textiles. The earliest metal made was **copper** for jewelry and simple tools. It was later heated to become more workable and was made into knives, axes, hoes, and weapons.

Around 3000 BCE, Mesopotamian metalworkers discovered a mixture, or alloy, of copper and tin that created a harder and stronger metal called **bronze.** Bronze was used to make weapons such as swords, spears, axes, shields, armor, and bronze-tipped plows for farming. Although copper is a fairly common ore, tin is relatively rare. Long-distance trade routes developed around the need for tin. Sometime around 1000 BCE, **iron** tools and weapons were first developed. Metalworkers discovered that when carbon was added to iron, it became much stronger. As iron is much more common than tin, it was more affordable to lower classes. Thus, changes occurred in warfare and, in some places like Greece, politics. Knowledge of metalworking spread all over Mesopotamia, the Mediterranean area, Africa, and Asia.

The exact origin of the **wheel** is unknown, but we do know that Sumerians used wheeled carts for several centuries before they were more formally organized around 3200 BCE. The wheel allowed for the transport of heavier loads and much longer distance travel and trade. This important technology spread rapidly and within a few centuries was the standard means of overland transport.

An Alternative Way of Life—Not Everyone Becomes a Farmer

Pastoral nomadism was another lifestyle that developed at this time. Pastoral nomads depended on their herd for survival and traveled to find grassland or **steppe** land required for their herds to graze.

Pastoral nomadism was not a step toward a life of farming. It was a complicated and advanced lifestyle in which nomads literally lived off their animals. Life could be quite difficult for these early pastoralists, and in response, they developed fighting skills, using both offensive and defensive military tactics to defend their herds.

❯ THE EARLIEST CIVILIZATIONS

Farming communities often developed along riverbanks. As the riverbanks flooded and carried silt onto the land, the soil became more fertile. The river also allowed for transportation and communication. Flood control and irrigation projects were soon developed. Such cooperation among these first civilizations led to the development of the first urban centers or cities. These large, densely populated, permanent settlements shared many common characteristics:

- Diverse people
- Specialization—people with different jobs
- Social stratification—some people had more status than others
- Trade

Early cities were larger than Neolithic towns and villages, had more intense specialization, professional craftsman, professional managers (such as governors and tax collectors), and professional cultural specialists (such as priests). Cities had a large economic center called the **marketplace,** which became the center of political, military, and economic control.

These cities often led to the growth of more complex societies. These societies often had the following in common:

- Food surplus
- Cities
- Specialization
- Trade
- Social stratification
- Organized government
- Complex religions
- Written language
- Arts/architecture

Mesopotamia

The "land between the waters" in southwest Asia is part of the **Fertile Crescent**, and was the site of one of the earliest farming communities. Small-scale irrigation started in Mesopotamia around 6000 BCE. By 3000 BCE, **Sumer** (as it came to be known) had a population of 100,000. Temples, public buildings, defensive walls, and irrigation systems were built by laborers recruited by government authorities.

Rulers were followed closely in status by the priests and priestesses. A noble class of warriors and judges advised the monarch. A fourth group was called the **free commoners**, who worked as farmers, builders, craftsmen, or professionals such as scribes. The **dependent clients**, a subgroup of commoners, owned no property and worked only on the estates of others. All commoners paid taxes with food surplus or labor. At the bottom of the social pyramid were the **slaves**, either prisoners of war or those serving punishment for debt crimes.

In Sumer, cities grew as they expanded their irrigation systems, eventually developing into city-states. A **city-state** is a sovereign city (meaning it makes its own laws and is not ruled by anyone else) that has a hinterland or adjoining lands that support it with agricultural goods. Sumerian city-states had distinctive step-shaped pyramids called **ziggurats** that were temples to the gods. Over time, these city-states were conquered and united into a single empire by many societies in succession—the Akkadians, Babylonians, Assyrians, and Persians, to name a few.

One of the most famous emperors of Mesopotamia was the Babylonian **Hammurabi** who ruled from 1792 to 1750 BCE. He is most famous for his legal code of laws, which he promulgated on stone stelae (or steles), or columns, throughout his empire; this was the first documented attempt in ancient history to detail crimes with specific punishments.

Hammurabi's code of laws had three main principles:

- Retribution, whereby a crime was punished by a like sentence ("an eye for an eye").
- Social standing determined punishment. The lower in social standing you were, the more severe your punishment. A commoner poking out the eye of a noble in a fight would be put to death.
- Government had a responsibility to its citizens. If your house was robbed and the thief was not caught, the local government would reimburse you.

Egypt

Around 5000 BCE, experimentation with agriculture began in the Nile River area with crops such as barley and wheat. Farmers soon built dikes to protect the fields from the floods. By 4000 BCE, villages had developed irrigation systems. The Nile protected Egypt from invasion, and so did the Red Sea, Mediterranean Sea, and Sahara Desert.

The most famous architecture of ancient Egypt includes the pyramids of Giza, which were built as tombs for pharaohs. The polytheistic Egyptians believed that the gods judged your life and that if found worthy, your spirit lived on in an afterlife. This belief led to the process of mummification and to elaborate tombs in whose walls the hieroglyphic accounts of the pharaohs' lives were written.

The Egyptians excelled in making bronze weapons and were skilled in mathematics, medicine, and astronomy. The solar calendar of 365 days that we use today was first devised in ancient Egypt. Around 3100 BCE, the Egyptians developed their own written language made up of pictographs, or **hieroglyphics.**

The pharaoh was at the top of the social class structure, followed by priests, commoners, and slaves. Egypt had professional military forces and many administrators and tax collectors. Unlike in Mesopotamia, women in Egypt, if they were literate, could often take on jobs as administrators, and there was even one woman pharaoh, **Hatshepsut.**

Indus Valley

This urbanized civilization developed between 3000 BCE and 2500 BCE. Its written language is still not understood, but we do know that its **polytheistic** religious belief system centered on a strong concern for fertility. The entire area was approximately 500,000 square miles, larger than both Mesopotamia and Egypt.

The two largest Indus Valley cities have been named **Harappa** and **Mohenjo-Daro.** These walled cities, designed in a grid pattern, featured broad streets, marketplaces, temples, assembly halls, public baths, and uniform housing, and even private bathrooms with showers. Indus Valley people traded pottery, tools, and decorative items; they obtained gold, silver, and copper from Persia and wool, leather, and olive oil from Mesopotamia. Metal tools of bronze and copper have been found, as well as jewelry made of precious stones. Cotton was cultivated in this area before 5000 BCE.

The writing system of this early civilization has yet to be deciphered. We do know that it used about 400 symbols to represent sounds and words. These symbols have been found on clay seals and copper tablets. Sometime after 2000 BCE, the Indus civilization was on the decline. A combination of environmental factors might have caused this, and by 1500 BCE, the civilization had collapsed.

Aryans

The Aryans, a nomadic people of Indo-European origin, entered the Indian subcontinent through the Khyber Pass around 1700 BCE. They quickly dominated the inhabitants of the Indus Valley and established a racial mix in what is now **India.** Aryans left a collection of sacred hymns, songs, prayers, and rituals known as the **Vedas.** They reveal a hierarchical, male-dominated society. The Aryans were polytheistic with many gods connected to nature. Their social structure had probably the largest impact on India; it gradually became the basis for the **caste system.**

People were divided into four **varnas** based on occupation and racial purity:
- Brahmins (scholars and priests)
- Kshatriyas (rulers and warriors)
- Vaishyas (merchants, farmers, craftsmen)
- Sudras (servants)

The lower class of **untouchables** (outcastes) was incorporated into the system later. Aryans tried to prohibit intermarriage between the varnas, but this was difficult to enforce, and over the years a blending of Aryan and indigenous people took place.

Shang and Zhou

The first river valley civilization in China developed along the **Huang He** or **Yellow River.** The dynasty that ruled this civilization is called the **Shang,** which ruled a northern territory from 1766 to 1122 BCE. Major archeological evidence used to prove the existence of the Shang dynasty is found in **"oracle bones."** The creation of written Chinese (pictograph) characters is traced back to the Shang.

The Shang developed **bronze metallurgy**, which helped in the development of a military state. The next and longer dynasty, the **Zhou** (1122 to 256 BCE), created the concept of the **Mandate of Heaven,** meaning power to rule was granted from heaven. Zhou society placed great emphasis on the **veneration of ancestors**. Additionally, in the Zhou period, **iron metallurgy** spread to China.

The Zhou lost control of their empire in the 5th century. This was followed by the Warring States Period, a time in which various noble families fought amongst each other for control of China. This period ended in 221 BCE with the rise of the Qin dynasty.

Mesoamerica and South America

In the Americas, agriculture developed around 1500 BCE, when the **Olmecs** settled along river banks in the coastal plain near the **Gulf of Mexico**. The first important settlement was **San Lorenzo,** which was the religious, political, and economic center for the Olmecs' large population. Later, **La Venta** served as an important center, and with its abundant rainfall, there was no need to build an extensive irrigation system. Olmec artisans carved masks and human figurines out of jade. One of the great mysteries of the Olmecs is the **Colossal Heads** they built, which are six feet high and weigh between 16 and 18 tons each. It is thought that they are carvings of leaders.

In South America, around 2500 BCE, cultivation of such crops as beans, peanuts, and sweet potatoes was occurring in the **Andean heartland.** Around 1000 BCE, an important religious cult—the **Chavin**—gained influence, and the society became more complex. Chavin de Huantar was the most important ceremonial center and had several large temple platforms. Artisans worked with ceramics, textiles, and gold. Both Mesoamerica and South America constructed religious shrines.

❯❯ DEVELOPMENT AND POPULARITY OF RELIGION

Early civilizations were mostly polytheistic. Often gods or goddesses were associated with nature, and sacrifices were made to these gods to ensure things such as good harvests. Around 600 BCE, major religions and philosophies emerged to address some new questions or concerns that the previous traditions may not have been sufficiently addressing. This period is called the **Axial Age.** The axial represents the core ideas around which a society revolves.

Axial Age in India

HINDUISM

The religion of Hinduism originated in India. It is a belief system that evolved over time and actually refers to a wide variety of beliefs and practices that developed in South Asia. Hinduism is often described as not just a religion but a way of life. At the most basic level, Hindus believe that they have a **dharma,** or duty, to perform in life. If all follow their dharma, the world works smoothly. This dharma is determined by birth and one's stage in life. If one follows his dharma, he will get good **karma.** It is the accumulation of this good karma (the sum of all good and bad deeds performed) that allows someone to move up in level of **samsara** in the next life.

Hindus believe that they will be **reincarnated** (reborn) after death. The new position they assume in the next life will depend on how well they performed their dharma in the past life. The ultimate goal for Hindus is to end the cycle of reincarnation by finally reaching **moksha** or oneness with the universe. Hinduism is a polytheistic religion that believes in Brahma, the creator god, and his various incarnations including Vishnu, Shiva, and Devi. Bhatki is a popular practice in which followers have a personal devotion to a particular deity.

The social structure known as the **caste system** has had an enormous impact on the followers of Hinduism. The four varnas are the basis for the caste system. A fifth group at the bottom of society became known as the **untouchables.** The caste system is based on the concepts of racial purity and pollution. To ensure purity, people should marry only members of their own caste.

BUDDHISM

Siddhartha Gautama, who lived from approximately 563 BCE to 483 BCE, became an important axial-age thinker in India. After meditating, he reached enlightenment and became known as the **Buddha (enlightened one).** The Buddha taught that there were **four noble truths:**

1. All life is suffering.
2. Suffering is caused by desire.
3. There is a way out of suffering.
4. The way out of suffering is to follow the Eightfold Path.

The **Eightfold Path** includes right understanding, purpose, speech, conduct, livelihood, effort, awareness, and concentration. The ultimate goal for Buddhists is to reach **nirvana,** which is the release from the cycles of reincarnation and the achievement of union with the universe. According to Buddhism, no one needs the rituals of Hinduism. Gods and goddesses are not necessary—everyone can seek enlightenment on his own, and no one is an outcast by birth.

Axial Age in China

From 600 BCE to 221 BCE, no strong central government control existed in China. This time of constant fighting and disorder is referred to as the **Era of Warring States.** It is within this time that three important philosophies emerged in China: **Confucianism, Daoism,** and **Legalism.**

CONFUCIANISM

Confucius (551 to 479 BCE) was a philosopher who believed the key to restoring peace was to find the right kind of leadership to rule China. His two most important concepts were **ren** (appropriate feelings) and **li** (correct actions), which must be used together in order to have any effect. Additionally, **filial piety** or respect for one's parents was a key concept.

Rulers would rule by **moral example,** and people would learn to behave properly through the example of those superior to them. In Confucianism there are **five key relationships:**

> ▶ AP EXPERT TIP
>
> Like many great religious leaders, Confucius did not write his knowledge down. Confucius's teachings were brought together by his disciples in a book called *The Analects.* Knowing the basic doctrines (books, poems, etc.) of the major religions is required by the AP exam.

1. Ruler to subject
2. Father to son
3. Husband to wife
4. Older brother to younger brother
5. Friend to friend

DAOISM

The **Tao te Ching** or **Dao te Ching,** a collection of Daoist wisdom, is attributed to Laozi, a Chinese sage. The literal translation of Dao is the **way,** the **way of nature,** or the **way of the cosmos.** According to Daoism, all life is interdependent, and human beings should exist in harmony with nature. Daoists taught the concept of **wu wei,** which means *act by not acting.*

Daoists believed it was useless to try to build institutions to govern humans, because institutions (or anything that rewarded knowledge) were dangerous. For Daoists, the ideal state is a small, self-sufficient town. The ultimate goal should be to cultivate the virtues of patience, selflessness, and concern for all. Daoism provided an escape from the proper behavior of Confucianism—it encouraged people to take time off, relax, just let things happen. Laozi gained many disciples in China, though some mixed his ideas with magic and attempted to search for immortality.

LEGALISM

The philosophy of Legalism was based on the principle that people were inherently evil and needed strict laws and punishment to behave properly. Additionally, a strong central government with an absolute leader and heavy taxes would ensure a more stable society.

Axial Age in the Middle East

JUDAISM

The Hebrews were a nomadic people who migrated out of Mesopotamia sometime around 2000 BCE and settled in the area known as Palestine. By 1700 BCE, many Hebrews had migrated into Egypt, and most were enslaved by the Egyptians. Sometime after 1300 BCE, Moses led the Hebrews out of Egypt in a flight that became known as the **Exodus.**

The Hebrews believed that they were protected by their own god **YHWH** (what may have been pronounced *Yahweh* but was considered too holy a word to say aloud). According to the Bible, the **Ten Commandments** were given to Moses by God. The Hebrews (who became known as Jews) established a **monotheistic tradition,** which claims there is one creator (God).

After the Exodus, the Hebrews returned to the "Promised Land" on the eastern shores of the Mediterranean, and the kingdom of **Israel** was established. The height of Israelite power came during the reigns of King David and his son Solomon around 1000 BCE. Later, the Assyrians invaded; the Babylonians then finished the job. Ultimately the former kingdom of Israel was swallowed up by the Greek and Roman Empires after 330 BCE. In 135 CE, the Romans drove the Jews out of their homeland; this is referred to as the **Diaspora.** Jews then survived in scattered communities around the Mediterranean region, Persia, and central Asia.

CHRISTIANITY

Jesus was born to Jewish parents about 4 BCE in the area know as **Judea** (today the country of Israel), which was part of the Roman Empire. Jesus taught devotion to God and love for fellow human beings. He earned a reputation for wisdom and the power to perform miracles. His message of the **Kingdom of God** alarmed authorities, however, and to quell a potential rebellion, they had him executed on a cross in the early 30s CE.

According to Jesus, men and women were considered spiritually equal before God. The faithful would experience **eternal life** in heaven with God. Jesus' followers believed that he rose from the dead and that he was the son of God. They compiled a body of writings about his life and his messages; this became the **New Testament.** The earliest followers of Jesus (Christians) were all Jews, but in the mid-first century CE, the disciple Paul began to spread the message of Jesus to non-Jews, or gentiles. He and other missionaries used the Roman roads and sea lanes to spread this new religion. However, Christians, like the Jews, refused to honor the state cults or to worship the emperor as a god and thus were often subject to campaigns of persecution.

Even so, the religion continued to spread throughout the empire, until Emperor Constantine issued the **Edict of Milan** in 313 CE, making Christianity legal in the Roman Empire. Emperor Theodosius went on to make it the official religion of the empire in 380 CE. Christianity also spread to Mesopotamia, Iran, and parts of India. Over time, the Southwest Asian Christians and the Western (or Roman) Christians grew apart. Southwest Asian Christians followed a form of the religion called **Nestorian Christianity.** This form of Christianity continued to spread across the Silk Roads into central Asia, India, and China. Another form of Christianity developed in Northern Africa and is called **Coptic Christianity** based on the Coptic language they used. Coptic Christian kingdoms have existed in Ethiopia since the sixth century, and the religion still thrives in Egypt and Ethiopia today.

Role of Women in Religion

- **Buddhism:** Women could achieve nirvana. An alternative lifestyle was available for women as nuns in a monastery.
- **Christianity:** Men and women were equal in eyes of God. Women could go to heaven. Many early converts were women. Women could live in convents.
- **Confucianism:** Men were superior to women. One of five key relationships is that of husband to wife.
- **Hinduism:** Men were superior to women. Women were not allowed to read the sacred prayers, the Vedas. In order to reach moksha, one must be a male Brahmin.

❯ CLASSICAL SOCIAL ORDER

Greece

POLITICAL DEVELOPMENT

Greece's political identity revolved around the concept of the **polis** or city-state. A few functioned as monarchies, but most were based on some form of collaborative rule. The two most famous city-states were **Sparta** and **Athens.** Sparta used military strength to impose order, while Athens used democratic principles to negotiate order. Athens's government was a direct democracy that relied on its small size and the intense participation of its citizens. Those citizens were free adult males. (This meant no women, foreigners, or slaves could be citizens.) The Spartans, on the other hand, lived life with no luxuries; social distinction was earned through discipline and military talent. Boys began their rigorous military training at age seven, and girls received physical education to promote the birth of strong children.

Greek cities in Anatolia (modern-day Turkey) resented what they viewed as the oppressive rule of the Persian Empire and revolted, starting the **Persian War** (500–470 BCE). Athenians sent their own troops in support. The alliance of the Greeks against the Persians led to the formation of the **Delian League,** of which Athens served as the leader. However, this leadership soon caused resentment in other parts of the Greek world. The conflict came to a head during the **Peloponnesian War** (431–404 BCE). Sparta and Athens led the two conflicting camps, and though Sparta was victorious, the internal conflict weakened Greece and left it vulnerable to domination by Macedonia, a frontier state north of the Greek peninsula.

King Philip II (359–336 BCE) of Macedon consolidated control of his kingdom, and by 338 BCE the region was under his control. His son **Alexander** conquered Persia by 330 BCE and went on to conquer most of the northwest regions of the Indian subcontinent. This led to the creation of a **Hellenistic Empire and Era.** The empire was divided among three of his generals: **Antigonid** (Greece and Macedonia), **Ptolemaic** (Egypt), and **Seleucid** (Persia). During the Hellenistic Era, caravan trade flourished from Persia to the West, and sea lanes were widely traveled throughout the Mediterranean Sea, Persian Gulf, and Arabian Sea.

SOCIAL STRUCTURE AND GENDER ROLES

Greece was a **patriarchal** society; women owned no land but could be priestesses. Literacy was common among upper-class Greek women, and Spartan women competed in athletics. Slaves were acquired because they had debt, had been taken as prisoners of war, or had been traded.

CULTURE, ARTS, SCIENCE, AND TECHNOLOGY

The Greeks stressed an appreciation of human beauty through religion, philosophy, art, architecture, literature, athletics, and science. **Polytheistic,** the Greeks believed that their gods were personifications of nature. The great ancient Greek philosopher **Socrates** encouraged reflection, and his student **Plato** wrote *The Republic* in which he described his ideal state ruled by a philosopher king. Plato's student **Aristotle** wrote on biology, physics, astronomy, politics, and ethics. Aristotle is considered the father of logic and deductive reasoning. The great epic poems attributed to Homer, *The Iliad* and *The Odyssey*, convey the value of the hero in Greek culture. In architecture, the Greeks built temples using pillars or columns, and they developed a realistic approach to sculpture. The Olympic Games were held regularly to demonstrate athletic excellence. The Greeks also made great strides in anatomy, astronomy, and math, including the medical writings of Galen and the mathematics of Archimedes.

India

POLITICAL DEVELOPMENT

Following the invasions of the Aryans, India by the sixth century BCE saw the development of **small regional kingdoms**, which often fought each other. Though there were periods of centralized rule, the subcontinent remained **decentralized** through most of its history.

> **▷ AP EXPERT TIP**
>
> *Centralized rule* means that the emperor rules directly through governors or military leaders or scholars. *Decentralized rule* means that the emperor lets local rulers rule their own people, although they must collect and pay taxes and/or tribute to the emperor. Centralized rule is often more stable and resistant to outside invaders.

One significant example of that centralized rule was that of the **Mauryans.** In the 320s BCE, **Chandragupta Maurya** successfully dominated the area and set up an administration to rule his empire. His grandson, **Ashoka,** continued his grandfather's conquering ways until the bloody campaign to conquer Kalinga. This bloodbath convinced Ashoka to stop using violence and instead rule by moral example using his Rock Edicts (carved into cliffs and in caves). During his reign, Ashoka set up a tightly organized bureaucracy, which collected taxes and was made up of officials, accountants, and soldiers. After Ashoka's death, the Mauryan Empire declined, and India returned to being a land of large regional kingdoms.

In 320 CE, Chandra Gupta (no relation to the other one) established the **Gupta Empire** and conquered many of the regional kingdoms. Instead of setting up an organized bureaucracy, the Guptas left the local government and administration in power. Under the Gupta, Hinduism again reasserted itself as the primary religion of Indian culture. Gupta rule continued until the invasion of the White Huns severely weakened the empire and India returned to regional rule.

ECONOMIC DEVELOPMENT

Ashoka encouraged agricultural development through irrigation and encouraged trade by building roads, hospitals, rest houses, wells, and inns along those roads. Agricultural surpluses led to an increase in the number of towns that maintained marketplaces. Overland trade via the **Silk Roads** connected India with China through central Asia. Indian sailors mastered the technique of riding the monsoon (seasonal) winds, and they sailed to Indonesia and Southeast Asia. Their goods, such as cotton and black pepper, made it all the way to Rome.

SOCIAL STRUCTURE AND GENDER ROLES

India developed into a **patriarchal** society; women were forbidden from reading the sacred prayers (the Vedas), and under Hindu law, they were legally minors and subject to the supervision of men. In order to marry well, a woman's family needed a large dowry. Women were not allowed to inherit property, and a widow was not permitted to remarry. The social structure became dominated by the power of the Brahmins and the caste system. As the Brahmins became more powerful, during the rule of the Guptas, caste distinctions grew.

CULTURE, ARTS, SCIENCE, TECHNOLOGY

India's culture thrived, as evidenced by its advancements in the arts, math, and science. The Mauryan emperor Ashoka became a devout Buddhist around 260 BCE, after the battle at Kalinga, and changed the way he ruled his empire. He rewarded Buddhists with land and encouraged the spread of the religion by building monasteries and stupas. He even sent out missionaries, who facilitated the spread of **Buddhism**. But through political support, **Hinduism** gradually eclipsed the influence of Buddhism. The Guptas gave land grants to Brahmins, supported education that promoted Hindu values, and built great temples in urban centers. Indian art during this time stressed symbolism rather than accurate representation. Math and science flourished in areas such as geometry and algebra. The circumference of the earth and the value of pi were calculated. Additionally, the concept of zero, the decimal system, and the number system we use today, called Arabic numbers, were developed.

China

POLITICAL DEVELOPMENT

China's political development began during the **Era of Warring States** (403–221 BCE). In 221 BCE, the first emperor, **Qin Shihuangdi**, ended the Era of Warring States through policies influenced by Legalism and started China's tradition of centralized imperial rule under the **Qin dynasty.** He had a centralized bureaucracy and divided the land into administrative provinces. For protection, he sponsored the building of defensive walls throughout the empire, which were the predecessor to China's **Great Wall.** Laws, currencies, weights, measures, and the Chinese script were standardized. The emperor had most Confucius books burned and had 460 scholars buried alive. His rule and dynasty lasted only 14 years, but he established the precedent for centralized imperial rule in China, which would last for 2,000 years. When the emperor died in 207 BCE, a new dynasty—the Han—was established.

The **Han dynasty** (207 BCE–220 CE) was much longer than the Qin dynasty. The most prominent emperor **Wu Di** (141–87 BCE) built roads and canals and established an imperial university with Confucianism for the curriculum. The university founded the **civil service exams,** which became the entry test for government jobs. In the Han dynasty, a foreign policy of expansion was pursued, and North Vietnam, Korea, and central Asia came under its control.

ECONOMIC DEVELOPMENT

China's economy was based on agriculture, and it flourished with the increase in long-distance trade. Iron metallurgy was introduced, which led to an increase in the military strength of the empire. It was during the Han dynasty that the trade route known as the **Silk Road** began to flourish. The route was a series of roads that allowed trade to connect the Han Empire with central Asia, India, and the Roman Empire.

The Han also followed a **tributary system of trade.** Officially, the policy was that the Han did not need to trade with their inferior neighbors, so instead they demanded tribute from neighboring groups and gave trade goods in return. In addition, the Han often sent gifts to nomad groups so as to deter invasion.

SOCIAL STRUCTURE AND GENDER ROLES

China had a **patriarchal** society; a woman's most important role was to make a proper marriage that would strengthen the family's alliances. Upper-class women were often tutored in writing, arts, and music, but overall women were legally subordinate to their fathers and their husbands.

Socially, the highest class was that of the **scholar–gentry**. These landowning families were often the only ones able to take the civil service exam, because preparation was very expensive. Most Chinese were peasants who worked the land. Merchants, who gained great wealth with the increase in trade, were considered socially inferior because they did not produce anything but rather lived off the labor of others.

CULTURE, ARTS, SCIENCE, TECHNOLOGY

In China, the family became the most important cultural and organizational unit in society. The **family** consisted both of its living members and its **ancestors**. Confucius's **filial piety**, respect or reverence for one's parents, was also very important. This was also a time of great invention and innovation. Agriculture was aided by the development of the wheelbarrow, while watermills were created to grind grain. The sternpost rudder and compass aided sea travel. Possibly most important was the invention of **paper**, which increased the availability of the written word.

Rome

POLITICAL DEVELOPMENT

In 509 BCE, the Roman nobility overthrew the Etruscan king, and what had been a monarchy became a **republic**—a government in which the people elect their representatives. The republic consisted of two consuls who were elected by an assembly that was dominated by the wealthy class, known as the **patricians**. The Senate, made up of patricians, advised these consuls.

This system of leadership created tension between the patricians and the common people, known as the **plebeians.** Eventually, the patricians granted the plebeians the right to elect tribunes, who had the right to veto patrician-made laws. When a civil or military crisis occurred, a dictator was appointed for six months. Rome expanded throughout the Italian peninsula and then the Mediterranean. It encountered a fierce competitor in the city of Carthage in North Africa. This competition led to the Punic Wars, which took place between 264 and 146 BCE. Rome sacked the city of Carthage, solidifying its domination of the Mediterranean.

As Rome expanded, it transitioned from a republic to a dictatorship. The Roman general **Julius Caesar** led the army in its conquest of Gaul and, in 46 BCE, made himself dictator. He centralized military functions and initiated large scale building projects. But the senators feared Caesar was becoming a tyrant and assassinated him. Octavian took over and, in 27 BCE, was given the title Augustus. The next 250 years were called the **Pax Romana**, or Roman Peace. Rome's system of law had begun in 450 BCE with the **Twelve Tables**.

ECONOMIC DEVELOPMENT

Some 60,000 miles of roads linked the empire's 100 million people, linking all regions of the empire for trade and communication. A **uniform currency** was used, and while **Latin** was the language of politics and the Romans, **Greek** was the *lingua franca* for trade throughout the Mediterranean. The cities had sewers, plumbing, public baths, and access to fresh water through aqueducts.

SOCIAL STRUCTURE AND GENDER ROLES

Rome was **patriarchal**; the eldest male, **pater familias**, ruled as head of the family. Roman law gave the pater familias authority to arrange marriage for the children and the right to sell them into slavery—or even execute them. Women's roles were in supervising domestic affairs. **Slaves**, one-third of the population by the second century CE, worked on large estates in the countryside or in the cities as domestic servants.

CULTURE, ARTS, SCIENCE, TECHNOLOGY

> **▶ AP EXPERT TIP**
>
> You should be able to compare various forms of labor throughout history: for example, which societies made extensive use of slaves (Greece and Rome) and which did not (India and China) and why.

Romans were polytheistic and believed that the gods intervened directly in their lives. The empire tolerated the cultural practices of its subjects—if they paid their taxes, did not rebel, and revered the emperors and Roman gods. The Jews, strict monotheists, were considered a problem, and various groups often tried to overthrow Roman rule. After a series of bloody rebellions in the first and second centuries CE, the Jews were completely defeated by the Romans and forced out of the city of Jerusalem—the start of the Jewish Diaspora (or scattering). The Christians were often also persecuted. However, the number of Christians continued to grow, and by 313 CE, Emperor Constantine issued the Edict of Milan, which legalized Christianity in the empire. By 380 CE, Emperor Theodosius proclaimed Christianity as Rome's official religion.

Roman architecture took its inspiration from Greece, making its columns and arches more ornate. Improvements in engineering, including the invention of concrete, allowed the Romans to build stadiums, public baths, temples, aqueducts, and a system of roads.

❖ FUNCTION OF COMMERCE IN CLASSICAL CIVILIZATION

The Han Empire secured the trade routes through Central Asia; India's Mauryan Empire's regional states were able to provide the necessary stability; and the Romans kept the Mediterranean Sea safe for travel. This security allowed for long-distance trade to thrive.

The **Silk Road** trade originated during a diplomatic mission to Central Asian by nomads during the Han Empire. The silk brought as gifts was very popular, as were the horses that the diplomats brought back. The trade route began in the east in **Changan**, went through Mongolia and Turkestan, and veered either north or south around the Taklamakan Desert. It branched southeast to India or through Central Asia, and finally to the eastern end of the Roman Empire. Caravan routes were traveled in stages, from one oasis town to the next.

The **Indian Ocean** trade went from Guangzhou in southern China through the South China Sea to the islands of Southeast Asia, India, the Arabian Sea, and the Persian Gulf. The principal players in the trade were Malay and Indian sailors. The **Mediterranean Sea** is sometimes referred to as the **Roman Lake,** because the Roman Empire surrounded the sea. Sea trade flowed from Syria to Spain to North Africa. The Romans kept their "lake" safe from pirates, which allowed trade to grow and enabled the transport of goods from one part of the empire to the other.

Goods That Traveled East to West	
silk	pearls
spices	coral
cotton	ivory

Goods That Traveled West to East
glassware
jewelry
bronze goods
wool and linen
olive oil
gold and silver bullion

Spread of Illness

During the second and third centuries CE, both the Han and Roman Empires suffered large-scale outbreaks of epidemic disease. Diseases such as smallpox, measles, and bubonic plague had a devastating effect because people did not have the immunity or the medicine to combat them. In the second century in the Roman Empire, the population dropped by 25 percent. The effects of these diseases caused great economic and social change. Trade within these empires declined, and their economies became more regionally focused.

❯❯ MIGRATION OF CULTURES

Bantu Migration

The migration of the Bantu people began around 2000 BCE, and by 1000 CE, the Bantu occupied most of sub-Saharan Africa. Resources were stretched to their limits as the population increased. As a result, groups of people began to leave their homelands (in modern-day Nigeria) to set up new agricultural settlements, and the process repeated itself slowly.

The Bantu people often intermarried with those they came in contact with, and these people often adopted the Bantu language and joined the Bantu society. Around 1000 BCE, the Bantus began to produce iron and iron tools, which enabled them to clear more land and expand agriculture. This led to an increase in population and more migration. Around 500 CE, the cultivation of bananas—which had made their way to Africa via the Indian Ocean trade—enabled the Bantus to expand into heavily forested regions and to continue this migration process. Migration led to an increase in the overall population of Africa—from 3.5 million in 400 BCE to 22 million in 1000 CE—and the spread of agriculture throughout much of Africa. Today there are over 500 distinct (though related) languages that can be traced back to the Bantus.

Polynesian Migration

Humans migrated to Australia around 60,000 years ago via watercraft that could travel the shallow seas. These people developed maritime technology and agricultural expertise and eventually established settlements in the islands of the Pacific Ocean. Beginning around 2000 BCE, the peoples who settled the Polynesian islands migrated to islands such as Vanuatu, Fiji, Samoa, and later Hawaii. Long-distance voyages were taken on double canoes with large triangular sails and a platform between the two hulls for shelter.

▶ **AP EXPERT TIP**

The city-state form of government is common throughout history. Sumeri, the Maya civilization, medieval Germany, East African Swahili, and arguably modern-day Singapore are all examples of city-states throughout history. Knowing the characteristics of this form of government and comparing historical examples is an example of the type of knowledge the AP exam may ask you to demonstrate.

Some scholars believe that this **settlement** was accidental and caused by sailors being blown off course, while others believe it was a planned colonization. As the migration spread, so did the cultivation of new food crops such as yams, taros, breadfruit, and bananas and the husbandry of domesticated animals such as dogs, pigs, and chickens. The Polynesian islands developed into hierarchical chiefdoms in which leadership was passed down to the eldest son and relatives served as the local aristocracy. Conflict between groups, as well as population pressure, often led to further migration to new islands. The cultures and languages of these widely dispersed islands often adapted and evolved differently.

❯ FALL OF ANCIENT EMPIRES

Han, 220 CE

- *Economic Reasons*: Scholar officials were often exempt from taxes, and many peasants fled from tax collectors to these estates. A severe reduction in tax revenue financially crippled the empire. Long-distance trade decreased, but the Chinese were self-sufficient and not severely affected.
- *Political Reasons*: The government was unable to check the power of the large private estate owners. The emperor heavily relied on the advice of his court officials and was often misinformed for their personal gain.
- *Social Reasons*: The population increase led to smaller family plots and the peasant class had increased difficulty paying taxes.
- *Role of Nomads*: The Xiongnu invaded, but only after the empire had already fallen. Nomadic invasions took place because the empire was no longer providing people with what they needed.

Western Rome, 476 CE

- *Economic Reasons*: The rich landowning class often resisted paying their taxes, and when the tax collectors did approach, they were driven away by the landowners' private armies. Also, the church land was not taxable. As the empire declined, so did trade because of unsafe roads. The drop in tax revenue and inflation crippled Rome's economy.
- *Political Reasons*: The government had trouble finding bureaucrats who could enforce the laws. Power struggles for the throne plagued the empire. From 235 to 284 CE, 25 out of 26 emperors died violent deaths. The division of the empire into two sections allowed the eastern portion to remain stronger, while the western portion weakened.
- *Social Reasons*: Plagues dramatically reduced the population, in particular the farming population.
- *Role of Nomads*: The Roman army could not defend against the movement of such nomadic groups as the Ostrogoths, Huns, and Visigoths. Rome was sacked by the Visigoths in 476 CE.

Gupta, 550 CE

- *Economic Reasons*: The government had great difficulty collecting enough taxes to pay the army to protect its borders.
- *Political Reasons*: The regional powers of the Guptas were allowed to keep much of their administrative power. They eventually grew more powerful than the central government.
- *Role of Nomads*: The government was too weak to defend against the nomadic invasions of the White Huns.

Also, environmental problems, such as siltation and deforestation, were subtle factors in the collapse of many empires. As agriculture spread, extensive irrigation systems and slash-and-burn farming all took a toll. Agriculture introduced new diseases by allowing for more standing water, creating a breeding ground for mosquitoes and malaria. Contact with cattle and pigs spread measles and smallpox. The bubonic plague spread as rats became common.

Practice Section

1. Which of the following is NOT a feature of the age 8000 BCE to 500 CE?

   (A) The growth of agriculture

   (B) The increase in world population

   (C) The use of metal tools

   (D) The creation of a writing system

   (E) The use of gunpowder technology

2. The transformation to an agriculturally based economy as a result of the Neolithic Revolution

   (A) was gradual over hundreds or thousands of years.

   (B) began in one section of the world and extended from there.

   (C) was simultaneously established throughout the world.

   (D) had little effect on the environment.

   (E) led to a decline in population.

3. Pastoral nomads are comparable to established farmers in that they both

   (A) cultivate crops.

   (B) domesticate livestock.

   (C) settle into broader communities.

   (D) have task specialization.

   (E) utilize a written language.

4. The Neolithic Revolution impacted gender roles in that

   (A) men and women's economic positions were considered equal.

   (B) work outside of the dwelling was more highly esteemed.

   (C) women no longer worked.

   (D) men fulfilled the only important economic function.

   (E) men continued to hunt, while women gathered.

5. The descriptions below relate to what culture?

   • Established cuneiform as a writing form.
   • Was organized into city-states.
   • Exercised Hammurabi's Code as the policy of law.

   (A) Egypt

   (B) Indus

   (C) Mesopotamia

   (D) Huang He

   (E) Olmecs

6. The Egyptians benefited from the Nile as the Chinese benefited from the

   (A) Tigris.

   (B) Euphrates.

   (C) Yellow.

   (D) Indus.

   (E) Ganges.

7. The Chinese concept of the Mandate of Heaven refers to

    (A) the authority granted to the ruler by religious deities.

    (B) the conviction that China was superior to the rest of humanity.

    (C) the emperor's responsibility to pass laws for his people.

    (D) the unlimited supremacy of the emperor.

    (E) the faith in many gods at once.

8. The Indus Valley culture is still somewhat of an enigma to archeologists because

    (A) the Aryans shattered everything that was left of that civilization.

    (B) its writing system has not been deciphered.

    (C) the small size of the society makes it difficult to excavate.

    (D) its separation from the rest of humanity restricted trade and distribution.

    (E) its spiritual viewpoints play no role in religion in India today.

9. The age called the "Era of Warring States" refers to

    (A) the nomadic attacks that ended the powerful Roman Empire.

    (B) the era of chaos in China before the unification under the Qin dynasty.

    (C) the evolution from republic to empire in Rome.

    (D) the rebellion that finished the sovereignty of the first emperor of China.

    (E) the time of rule in India during which only local kingdoms held authority.

10. What concepts do Hinduism and Buddhism share?

    (A) Universal salvation

    (B) Reincarnation

    (C) The caste system

    (D) Monotheism

    (E) Heaven and hell

11. Which of the following pairs of historical figures did NOT impact the same region?

    (A) Confucius and Laozi

    (B) Ashoka and Siddhartha Gautama

    (C) Socrates and Alexander

    (D) Wu Di and Chandra Gupta

    (E) Constantine and Jesus

12. The Mauryan and Gupta Empires experienced India's

    (A) long and steady record of imperial rule.

    (B) pause in its political authority marked by regional kingdoms.

    (C) impressive influence of Islamic laws and culture.

    (D) history of conquest by nomadic invaders.

    (E) consistent imperial strengthening of Hindu principles.

13. Which sentence most precisely compares the fall of the Han and Roman Empires?

    (A) Both empires were seriously hurt by the decrease in trade.

    (B) Nomadic attacks were more of a detriment in Han than in Rome.

    (C) Imperial authorities demonstrated more power than local leaders.

    (D) Politicians were assassinated in both empires.

    (E) Rich landowners successfully eluded tax collectors.

14. Long-distance trade thrived in the classical empires because

    (A) many merchants were able to travel the whole length of the Silk Road.

    (B) government authorities kept trade routes protected and safe.

    (C) Chinese emissaries negotiated with Roman officials.

    (D) India stayed centrally ruled during the classical era.

    (E) the creation and use of the compass aided voyages.

15. Which two religions gave women a possible path to spiritual salvation?

    (A) Daoism and Christianity

    (B) Confucianism and Buddhism

    (C) Daoism and Confucianism

    (D) Buddhism and Christianity

    (E) Confucianism and Judaism

16. Both Greek and Chinese cultures had a

    (A) reliance on slavery for labor.

    (B) malleable social structure.

    (C) continuous dynastic sequence.

    (D) strict patriarchal family structure.

    (E) decentralized political organization.

17. Which of the following statements is accurate of both the Qin and Han dynasties?

    (A) Confucianism was the philosophical foundation of the law.

    (B) The merchant class was much respected.

    (C) The central government was powerful.

    (D) Trade was discouraged and sometimes forbidden.

    (E) Buddhism impacted both empires.

18. Which of the following civilizations encouraged citizen participation in government?

    (A) China

    (B) India

    (C) Persia

    (D) Egypt

    (E) Rome

19. Which of the following was NOT an issue in the Bantu migrations?

    (A) Population strains

    (B) Utilization of iron tools

    (C) Cultivation of bananas

    (D) Growth of agriculture

    (E) Desertification

20. Which of the following is NOT a feature of early human populations?

    (A) Diverse races

    (B) Work specialization

    (C) Social structures involving hierarchies

    (D) Trade

    (E) Representative government

Answers and Explanations

1. E

The spread of agriculture, growth in human population, use of metal technology, and writing all occurred during this time. However, the use of gunpowder technology did not begin until the period 600 to 1450 CE, during the Song dynasty in China.

2. A

The Neolithic Revolution was a gradual process that probably began with experimentation with seeds. Farming developed slowly over a long period of time.

3. B

Both pastoral nomads and settled farmers depend on the domestication of animals for their financial survival.

4. B

The expansion of farming led to a division of labor. Work that was performed outside the home was considered more important than domestic work conducted inside the home.

5. C

Mesopotamia developed cuneiform as a writing system, was divided into city-states, and used Hammurabi's Code as the system of law. (Hammurabi was an important ruler of the area.) Of the possible answers, this is the only society that used cuneiform. Egypt used hieroglyphics.

6. C

Early Chinese cultures grew along the Yellow, or Huang He River. The Tigris and Euphrates were in Mesopotamia. The Indus River and the Ganges River are in India.

7. A

The Mandate of Heaven is the belief that the gods have approved giving supremacy to the ruler, but that authority can also be taken away. Definite signs that indicate the loss of the mandate are floods, peasant rebellions, and nomadic attacks.

8. B

While the Indus civilization was discovered in the early 1900s, the writing system found on clay seals has yet to be decoded.

9. B

The Era of Warring States was a period of hundreds of years when no one state could control China; instead the smaller states fought each other for power.

10. B

The rebirth of the soul, or reincarnation, is fundamental principle of both Hindus and Buddhists, who both believe that it takes several lifetimes to amass the required amount of karma to be freed from the cycle of rebirth.

11. D

Wu Di was an emperor of the Han dynasty in China (East Asia). Chandra Gupta was the first ruler of the Mauryan Empire in India (South Asia).

12. B

Most of India's history features a decentralized government of provincial kingdoms. Both the Mauryan and Gupta Empires were effectively empowered to centralize significant areas of the Indian subcontinent.

13. E

Neither the Han nor the Roman Empire was capable of collecting sufficient tax funds. In both situations, large landowners avoided paying taxes. They often provided refuge to peasants on their land who were trying to escape the tax collectors as well.

14. B

If trade routes were protected and well maintained, long-distance trade flourished. Often when imperial rule was weak, roads were not kept in shape very long. Travel became unsafe, and trade declined as a consequence.

15. D
Both Buddhism and Christianity professed that women and men had equal access to salvation, though their equality here on earth was not guaranteed.

16. D
Both Greek and Chinese classical civilizations were patriarchal: Men were deemed the head of the household and, therefore, the most respected part of society.

17. C
The Qin used a strict Legalist attitude to rule, while the Han placed a strong weight on Confucianism. However, in order to keep their empires organized, both societies used a strict central government with an authoritative emperor.

18. E
In the beginning of the Roman Empire, the government was a republic, meaning that the citizens elected representatives to make decrees for them. Rome had a senate, which approved laws for its people, but as the city developed into an empire, the senate lost most of its control to an emperor.

19. E
The development of agriculture led to population increase, which contributed to the Bantu migration. Also, the use of iron tools allowed for more land to be obtainable for cultivation, which in turn resulted in more population growth. Finally, the cultivation of bananas enabled people to move into new areas and develop new diets.

20. E
Representative government was not a characteristic of the world's first civilizations. Most of these societies were governed by a small elite class who were usually relatively wealthy.

CHAPTER 2

Regional Interactions (600 to 1450 CE)

❯❯ A THUMBNAIL VIEW

- As in the previous chapter, this time period witnessed a tremendous growth in long-distance trade due to improvements in technology. Trade through the Silk Road, the Indian Ocean, the trans-Saharan trade route, and the Mediterranean Sea led to the spread of ideas, religions, and technology. During the period known as Pax Mongolia, when peace and order were established in Eurasia due to the vast Mongol Empire, trade and cultural interaction were at their height.

> ❯ **AP EXPERT TIP**
>
> When you are reading about a given situation, try to visualize where in the world those developments are taking place. Alternatively, reproduce a blank world map and take notes in the proper geographic region as you read.

- Major technological developments such as the compass, improved ship-building technology, and gunpowder shaped the development of the world.

- The movement of people greatly altered our world. Nomadic groups such as the Turks, Mongols, and Vikings, for instance, interacted with settled people—often because of their technology—leading to further change and development. One of the worst epidemic diseases in history, the bubonic plague (or Black Death), spread during this period due to the movement of people and their increased interaction.

- Religions such as Islam, Christianity, and Buddhism promoted the equality of all believers in the eyes of God. And though patriarchal values continued to dominate, the monastic life available in Buddhism and Christianity offered an alternative path for women.

- The spread of religion aided by the increase in trade often acted as a unifying force, though it sometimes caused conflict. Christianity and the Church served as the centralizing force in Western Europe, and throughout East Asia, the spread of Confucianism and Buddhism solidified a cultural identity. The new religion of Islam created a cultural world known as dar-al Islam, which transcended political boundaries.

- The political structures of many areas adapted and changed in response to the new conditions of the world. Centralized empires like the Byzantine, the Arab Caliphates, and the Tang and Song dynasties built on the successful models of the past, while decentralized areas (Western Europe and Japan) developed political organizations that more effectively dealt with their specific conditions. The movements of the Mongols altered much of Asia's political structure for a time, and recovery from that Mongol period introduced political structures that defined many areas for centuries to follow.

❯❯ POST-CLASSICAL CHINA

Tang Dynasty (618 to 907 CE)

POLITICAL DEVELOPMENT

Following the fall of the Han dynasty, China returned to rule by regional small kingdoms for the next 400 years. It was not until 581 CE that the Sui dynasty emerged, using Buddhism and the Confucian civil service system to establish legitimacy. The Sui dynasty started the construction of the Grand Canal and launched numerous campaigns to expand the empire. Rebellions overthrew the Sui in 618.

The Tang dynasty that followed was more focused on scholars than on soldiers. It did, however, expand its territory beyond China proper to Tibet and Korea. It also completed the Grand Canal and offered support to Buddhism, Daoism, and Confucianism. The capital, Changan, was a major political center, which foreign diplomats visited from the Byzantine and Arab worlds. In the middle of the eighth century CE, Tang power declined as higher taxes created tension within the population. Peasant rebellions led to more independent regional rule and to the abdication of the emperor. After this, there was a period of rule by regional warlords for the next 50 years.

ECONOMIC DEVELOPMENT

The dynasty established military garrisons, which allowed for the protection and security of **Silk Road** trade. An **equal field system** was established in which all peasants were given land in return for tax in grain and unpaid labor; at death they were to return the land to the government.

Changan was a major trading center and cosmopolitan city. The West Market there flourished with Indian, Iranian, Syrian, and Arab traders and their goods. By 640 CE, its population reached 2 million, making it the largest city in the world. Neighbors, such as Japan or Siam, became tributary states to China.

CULTURAL DEVELOPMENT

Culturally, the Tang dynasty was heavily influenced by the spread of **Buddhism**. **Empress Wu** started a school dedicated to Buddhist and Confucian scholarship and art.

Toward the end of the dynasty, Buddhism, a "foreign religion," was attacked for its economic and political power. From 841 to 845 CE, an **anti-Buddhist campaign** destroyed many monasteries. In the wake of this backlash, neo-Confucianism developed: Confucian scholars wanted a new form of Confucianism that would limit foreign influence. The result was an integration of Buddhist and Confucian ideas. Some ideas included individual self-improvement, the goodness of human beings, and the goal to strive and perfect oneself.

Women's marriages during the Tang dynasty were arranged within their own social class, but upper-class women could own property, move about in public, and even remarry. Poetry flourished with such poets as **Li Bai** and **Du Fu.**

Song Dynasty (960 to 1279 CE)

POLITICAL DEVELOPMENT

By 960 CE, the Song dynasty had re-established centralized control over China. The civil service exam system retained great prominence, successfully checking the power of the aristocracy. The Song de-emphasized a military approach and instead re-established the **tribute system** with its nomad neighbors. This involved "paying off" the nomads with such gifts as bolts of silk to keep the peace.

The Song, however, experienced military and economic problems. The scholar-controlled professional army was often ineffective, and too much paper money in circulation caused inflation. By 1126 CE, they had lost the northern half of the empire to nomads. The Southern Song continued to flourish until 1274, but military threats continued, and finally the greatest of all northern groups invaded in the 1200s, absorbing the Song dynasty into the new Mongol Empire.

ECONOMIC DEVELOPMENT

Rice production doubled due to new fast-ripening rice from Champa. Internal trade from the Yellow Sea and Grand Canal flourished due to the increased number of merchants and the growth in population. The capital of Kaifeng became a **manufacturing center** with its production of cannons, movable type printing, water-powered mills, looms, and high-quality porcelain. China had more per capita production than any other country in the world. Minted copper coins were used as money and eventually were replaced with paper currency. Officials collected taxes in cash—not goods—and letters of credit (known as flying cash) were used by merchants.

The Southern Song established their capital at **Hangzhou**, and commerce soared. With their cotton sails and **magnetic compasses**, the Song had the most powerful navy in the world. As a result, the dynasty's power shifted from the north to the south, and the Song became leaders in trade. Song goods made their way to Southeast Asia, India, Persia, and East Africa.

CULTURAL DEVELOPMENT

During the Song dynasty, women were entitled to keep their dowries and had access to jobs as merchants, but they also were subject to a practice called **foot binding.** The practice originated with the aristocratic class and was viewed as a sign of wealth and status. Girls as young as six had their feet bound in order to secure a better marriage.

Tang and Song Innovations

- The first use of the compass to aid maritime navigation
- A water-powered clock, demonstrating facility in mechanical engineering
- The invention of gunpowder—first demonstrated during the late 1000s CE, the explosive combination of sulfur and saltpeter would alter weapons technology forever and lead to the first cannons, rockets, and incendiary bombs.
- Philosophy—neo-Confucian thought delved into ancient texts and further codified traditional Chinese philosophy; it blended Confucianism with elements of Daoism and Buddhism.
- A printing press with movable type
- Stylized and symbolic landscape painting
- Paper money, letters of credit (flying cash)

❯❯ JAPAN (around 800 to 1200 CE)

POLITICAL DEVELOPMENT

Japan's geography as a group of islands led to the development of small isolated, independent communities. Clan members cooperated with each other much like a large, extended family. By the 600s, the Yamato clan had religious and cultural influence over other clans and wanted to copy China's model of empire building. Its leaders began to call themselves **emperors of Japan.** The Fujiwara clan, which dominated between the ninth and twelfth centuries CE, sent emissaries to China and modeled their capital, Nara, on Changan. They could not, however, successfully introduce a Chinese-style bureaucracy, and a strict hereditary hierarchy developed instead.

During the Kamakura Shogunate (1185–1333 CE), the emperor and his court kept their capital in Kyoto, yet a military dictatorship existed, ruled by powerful landholding clans. A Japanese form of **feudalism** developed in which the **Shogun**—supreme general—controlled the centralized military government and divided the land into regional units based on military power. The regional military leaders were the **daimyo,** and the warriors who fought for them were the **samurai.** Over the centuries, the samurai military class developed a strict warrior code called *bushido*. The emperor remained in power throughout this period, but served only as a symbolic figurehead. Many Shoguns were overthrown but the emperor was not.

ECONOMIC DEVELOPMENT

Japan was a predominantly agrarian society with a local artisan class of weavers, carpenters, and ironworkers. Trade and manufacturing developed more in the Kamakura Period, when it focused on markets in larger towns and foreign trade with Korea and China. Most people were peasants who worked on land that was owned by a lord or by Buddhist monasteries. Though their freedom was limited, peasants could keep what was left of their harvest after paying their tax quota. Those unable to pay their taxes became landless laborers known as **genin** and could be bought and sold with the land.

CULTURAL DEVELOPMENT

Japan adopted many foreign ideas but remained culturally true to its own traditions. According to **Shinto,** the religion native to Japan, everything possesses a spirit, or **kami**. Natural forces and nature were awe-inspiring, and shrines were built to honor kami. The first ruler from the **Yamato** clan claimed descent from the supreme Shinto deity, the Sun Goddess. Japan was also strongly influenced by Korea and China. It adopted Chinese technology, Chinese script, and Buddhism (though Japan developed its own version of Buddhism, which added a strong aesthetic dimension, known as **Zen Buddhism**). In the **Heian** period (794 to 1185 CE), contact with China was cut off, and the culture turned to expressing Japanese values.

Participating in a lavish court lifestyle, women dominated literature. *The Tale of Genji*, for instance, was written by Lady Murasaki. Wives inherited land from their husbands and often owned land, and priestesses dominated religious life. Over time, though, women lost power and influence.

❯ ISLAMIC CALIPHATES

Islam: The Religion

Prior to the spread of Islam, Arabs lived in separate, loyal, tribal groups and were often involved in overland and maritime trade. The city of Mecca later developed into an important religious site with a large influx of traders and pilgrims. The **Kaaba,** a black meteorite placed in the Great Mosque by Abraham, was in the center of the city, and most people worshipped idols.

Muhammad was born in 570 CE in Mecca. When he was 40, the angel Gabriel appeared to him and revealed that he had been selected to receive a divine message that there was only one all-powerful and all-knowing God, **Allah,** and that Muhammad was to be God's messenger. Muhammad preached that all people were to submit to Allah and that everyone was equal in the eyes of Allah. Muhammad's message was not met with enthusiasm in Mecca, and he fled to Medina in 622 CE, a journey known as the **hegira**. In Medina, he was viewed as a prophet and a political leader. Muhammad taught that he was the last of a long line of prophets from the Jewish and Christian scriptures that included Abraham, Moses, David, and Jesus. In 630 CE, he and his followers returned to **Mecca,** captured the city, and destroyed religious idols. After his death, Muhammad's revelations were written down by his followers in the **Quran**. The word *Islam* means "submission to God's will". Islam is a **universal religion** that is open to everyone.

Islam appealed to women because they had equal status to men before God, they could keep their dowries as wives, and there was a prohibition on female infanticide.

POLITICAL DEVELOPMENT

By the time of Muhammad's death, almost all of Arabia was under Islamic control. There was disagreement, however, over his successor. One group, the **Shia**, believed that the leader should be a descendant of Muhammad. The other group, the **Sunni**, preferred the community of Muslims to determine who would succeed him. The leader of the Muslims, the **caliph**, was both a political and spiritual leader.

After the first four caliphs, the **Umayyad clan** took control in 661 CE and transformed the caliphate into a hereditary monarchy, with its government centered in **Damascus**. They continued on to conquer Syria, Egypt, Persia, and Byzantine territory in West Asia, North Africa, and Spain. Their military skills, the soldiers' commitment to Islam, and the promise of plunder helped them in these conquests. The Umayyad Caliphate set up a bureaucratic structure in which local administrators governed their areas. All cultures were tolerated as long as people obeyed the rules, paid their taxes, and did not revolt. Arabic became the language of administration, business, law, and trade. The **Abbasid clan** overthrew the Umayyad dynasty in 750 CE and moved the capital of the empire to Baghdad, a political center and the second largest city in the world next to Changan.

> ### Five Pillars of Islam
>
> 1. Statement of faith: There is no God but Allah, and Muhammad is his messenger.
> 2. Pray five times a day facing Mecca.
> 3. Give alms (charity) to the poor.
> 4. Fast during the holy month of Ramadan.
> 5. Make a pilgrimage, or hajj, to Mecca during one's lifetime if able.

Eventually, the only remaining Umayyad prince settled in Spain and established a separate caliphate there. Berber tribesmen controlled much of the northern African coast, and the Mamluks revolted and gained control over Egypt from 1250 to 1517 CE. The term **Dar al-Islam**, or "all under Islam," refers to those areas in which a Muslim is welcome.

ECONOMIC DEVELOPMENT

Trade flourished throughout the caliphate and improved irrigation led to productive agriculture and an increase in tax revenues. Artisans flourished in the cities, making pottery, fabrics, and rugs. Paper was imported from China, and soon paper mills were set up. The vast Islamic empires also spread many types of agriculture, including sugarcane, citrus fruits, and coffee. Islam spread to West Africa through trans-Saharan trade, to East Africa and Southeast Asia through Indian Ocean trade, to Central Asia and China along the Silk Road, and to India through the migrations of the Turks.

CULTURAL DEVELOPMENT

Mosques, hospitals, schools, and orphanages were built throughout the empire. Intellectual achievements included the development of algebra, the concept of longitude and latitude, and the study of Greek philosophers such as Aristotle. **The House of Wisdom,** built in Baghdad in 830 CE, obtained Greek and Persian texts and translated them into Arabic. In art and architecture, the use of images was forbidden; instead, geometry and calligraphy were used to beautiful effect.

Byzantine Empire (300 to 1453 CE)

POLITICAL DEVELOPMENT

The Byzantine Empire, a continuation of the **Eastern Roman Empire,** was the only survivor from the classical age. The Roman Empire had officially been divided in 375 CE, with the western half severely weakened because the east produced the majority of grain and controlled the major trade routes. **Emperor Justinian,** who ruled from 527 to

565 CE, tried unsuccessfully to reconquer Western Rome. His *Body of Civil Law* **(Justinian's Code)** was written, and he replaced Latin with Greek as the official language of the empire. The central government was a hereditary monarchy. It made law, had an efficient military, oversaw effective land distribution, and had a bureaucracy that answered to the emperor. The emperor was considered a co-ruler with Christ and appointed the patriarch. Military generals were appointed to rule, and free peasants were given land for military service.

ECONOMIC DEVELOPMENT

Its location on the Mediterranean Sea contributed to strong trade in the Byzantine Empire. Silkworms were smuggled out of China, which allowed a Byzantine silk industry to develop. Artisans produced glassware, linen, jewelry, and gold and silver work.

CULTURAL DEVELOPMENT

Most people spoke Greek. In theory, there was social mobility through the bureaucracy, army, trade, or service to the Church, but in reality, mobility was limited. Constantinople was the political and intellectual center, with libraries containing Greek, Latin, Persian, and Hebrew texts.

The Byzantine and Roman Christian churches had been growing apart since the fall of Rome, and a disagreement over the worship of icons—images of saints—was the final straw. The Pope and the Patriarch excommunicated each other, and in 1054 CE, the church officially split into the **Roman Catholic Church** and the **Eastern Orthodox Church.** This Eastern Orthodox form of Christianity later spread to the Slavic people and Russia.

❱❱ DECENTRALIZED STATES IN EUROPE

Western Europe—Early Middle Ages (around 500 to 1000 CE)

POLITICAL DEVELOPMENT

Western Europe remained politically decentralized. The Franks came closest to re-establishing imperial control with the leadership of Clovis and, later, the Carolingian Empire of **Charlemagne**. Europe developed a **feudal system** in which land was given to vassals in exchange for military service, allowing them to gain power. The centralizing power during this period was the Church, and by the 13th century, the Church owned one-third of all the land in Europe.

ECONOMIC DEVELOPMENT

During this time, peasants became **serfs**; they had the right to work a portion of the land and could pass that right on to their children, but they could not leave the land. They could keep a portion of what they grew, but the majority of their earnings went to the lord. Serfs paid taxes for use of the lord's mill, had to work on the lord's lands, and had to provide gifts on holidays. These estates became large walled **manors** that were economically self-sufficient. They maintained mills, bakeries, and breweries. They had their own private armies served by armor-clad knights. The introduction of the heavy plow led to an increase in agricultural production.

CULTURAL DEVELOPMENT

Birth was the determining factor of one's status, and marriage was the key to political power. Christian nunneries were a way for women to escape their traditional duties and exercise leadership. Beginning in the 12th century, the code of conduct called chivalry developed. It stressed honor, modesty, loyalty, and duty. Monasteries were the dominant feature of social and cultural life, and they often had large landholdings. Monks preserved classical knowledge by hand-copying great literature and philosophical works.

▸ NOMADIC CULTURES

Vikings (Dates of Influence—around 800 to 1100 CE)

The Vikings were a nomadic group who had settled in present day Scandinavia. In order to supplement their farm production, they conducted seasonal raids into Europe and ransacked towns. Using small and maneuverable boats, they terrorized coastal communities in France, Scotland, Ireland, and England. The Vikings eventually evolved from plunderers into traders and established communities in Scotland, northern France, and Eastern Europe. Scandinavia was gradually Christianized during this period.

These outstanding seafarers also traded actively throughout the North Sea and Baltic Sea. In the 800s, they colonized Iceland and Greenland, and around 1000 CE, they established a colony that lasted only a few decades in Newfoundland, modern Canada. The transplanted Viking settlements in France became known as Normans (or **"Northmen"**). In 1066 CE, a Norman lord named William from northern France invaded England with his army. He defeated the Saxons and established Norman power in what is now Britain.

Turks (Dates of Influence—around 1000 to 1450 CE)

The Turks, a pastoral nomadic group from the **central Asian steppes**, began gradually to migrate out of the steppes at the end of the first millennium. They were often hired by Muslim leaders as mercenaries, or hired soldiers. The **Seljuk Turks,** who had converted to Islam, invaded Abbasid territory and captured Baghdad in 1055. The caliph was left as the spiritual authority of the empire, but the Seljuk Sultan became the secular monarch. By 1071 CE, they defeated the Byzantine Empire and took most of Anatolia (modern-day Turkey).

The **Afghan Turks** were nomads from Afghanistan and began a series of raids into India in the 10th century. They looted cities for gold and jewels and destroyed Hindu temples and then left. It wasn't until the 12th century that they invaded and then started to govern. This started the **Delhi Sultanate,** which ruled northern India from 1206 to 1526 CE. These Turks introduced a strong Muslim presence in India.

Mongols (Dates of Influence—around 1200 to 1550 CE)

A second pastoral nomadic group from the central Asian steppes, the Mongols would go on to create the world's largest empire. These nomadic herders' lives revolved around their sheep, goats, and yaks for food, clothing, and shelter; their camels for transportation; and their horses for mobility. This clan-based society was organized around bloodlines. **Genghis Khan** successfully united the various Mongol tribes, and their greatest strength was their **mobility** and military power. Once united, Genghis led his troops into Central Asia, Tibet, northern China, and Persia. In 1215 CE, the Mongols attacked and destroyed present-day Beijing. The Mongol charge continued into Afghanistan and Persia, yet by 1227 CE, the Great Khan died, and his empire was divided amongst his four sons.

CHINA: THE YUAN DYNASTY

In 1276 CE, Genghis Khan's grandson, **Kublai Khan,** defeated the Southern Song dynasty, and for the first time, China was under foreign rule. Khan created a Chinese-style dynasty, adopting the Chinese name Yuan for it, with a fixed and regular tax payment system and a strong central government. Foreigners, not Chinese, were employed in the bureaucracy, and the civil service exam was not used. The Chinese were subject to different laws and were separated from the Mongols.

Connecting Beijing to Vienna was a communication system using horse relays and 1,400 postal stations. In time, overland and maritime trade flourished, and though the Mongols were not directly involved in the trade, they welcomed merchants and foreigners. Merchants converted their foreign currency to paper money when they crossed into China.

THE MIDDLE EAST: THE ILKHANATES

In 1258 CE, Kublai's brother, **Hulegu,** defeated the Abbasid Caliphate. The Mongols in the Middle East employed local bureaucrats in the government and converted to Islam by 1295 CE. The local rulers were permitted to rule, as long as they delivered the tax revenue and maintained order. Though they did not support agriculture, they did facilitate trade, and Mongol culture often mixed with that of the conquered people.

As the Mongols continued west, they met with their first and only major defeat. The armies of the **Mamluks,** a slave dynasty in Egypt, defeated the Mongols in 1260 CE and stopped the movement of the Mongols in that region.

RUSSIA: THE GOLDEN HORDE

The Mongol ruler **Batu** conquered and ruled Russia but kept a large number of the local rulers in power. The taxes on the peasants were heavy, but they were collected by Russian bureaucrats. Trade was supported, and although these Mongols were Muslim and conversion was encouraged, Christian missionaries were allowed to visit.

PAX MONGOLIA

At the peak of Mongolian power, with huge areas of Asia and Europe under one rule, there was a period called the **Mongol Peace.** For about a century, Mongol rule united two continents and allowed for relatively safe trade and contacts between very different cultures. It did so by eliminating tariffs. During this period, the **Silk Road trade** reached its greatest height. Paper money—a Chinese innovation—was used in many parts of the empire. It was also common for the Mongols to convert to or adopt the local religions, or at least be religiously tolerant.

MONGOL DECLINE

In 1274 and 1281 CE, the Mongols tried again to expand their empire—they invaded Japan. Typhoon winds destroyed their fleet both times, however. The Japanese believed these "kamikaze," or "sacred winds," had protected them. Despite great military accomplishment, the Mongol Empire lasted hardly three or four generations. While the Mongols were successful conquerors, they were poor administrators. Overspending led to inflation in different corners of the empire, and after the death of Kublai, leadership was weak and ineffectual. Rivalry among the successors of the great Khan further destabilized the empire, and the vast domain was divided among various generals. By 1350 CE, most of the Mongols' huge territory had been reconquered by other armies.

❯❯ RESULTS OF MIGRATION AND COMMUNICATION

West African Kingdoms

The introduction of the domesticated camel allowed for an increased flow of trade across the Sahara Desert, and as a result, Muslim and North African merchants began to establish commercial relations with West Africa.

Ghana (around 500 to 1200 CE)

Ghana was a regional state around the 400s or 500s CE, and an increase in **trans-Saharan trade** led to its growth in power and influence. By 800 CE the many farming villages in the area were united to create the kingdom of Ghana. It became an important commercial site and a center for trade in gold from the south, which it controlled and taxed. In return, it received ivory, slaves, horses, cloth, and salt. As Ghana's wealth increased, it built an army funded by the tax on trade. In the 900s CE, the kings converted to **Islam,** which led to improved relations with Muslim merchants. Islam was not forced on the people, however, and traditional animistic beliefs continued to be important. Those who engaged in trade often converted to Islam. After 1000 CE, Ghana found itself under assault from northern Berbers and other tribal groups nearby. It was eventually absorbed by the West African kingdom of Mali.

Mali (1235 to late 1400s CE)

The trans-Saharan trade in gold and salt continued to increase. Mali controlled and taxed all trade. The rulers honored Islam and provided protection and lodging for merchants. The **Sundiata** is an epic poem that tells how the first Mali emperor came to power; it was composed and recited by Mali **griots** or storytellers. The most famous Mali emperor was **Mansa Musa,** who ruled from 1312 to 1337. He built libraries, Islamic schools, and mosques throughout the kingdom. **Timbuktu** was the political capital and a regional cultural center of Islamic studies and art for all of West Africa. After 1350 CE, provinces began to assert their independence.

Christianity in North and East Africa

There remained a strong Christian tradition in **Egypt** and **Ethiopia.** There is a strong monastic strain in both Ethiopian and Egyptian (**Coptic**) Christianity. With the coming of Islam, Christians were still allowed to worship freely, and a unique linguistic expression of Christianity emerged.

East African City-States (around 900 to 1500 CE)

As the trans-Saharan trade was to West Africa, the **Indian Ocean trade** was to East Africa. Bantu people had settled on the coast, and Arabic merchants who traded along the East African coast interacted to create such East African city-states as **Mogadishu, Kilwa,** and **Sofala.** These states are often referred to as **Swahili city-states,** named for their language, which was a blend of Bantu and Arabic. In the 900s, Islamic merchants traded gold, slaves, and ivory for pottery, glass, and textiles from Persia, India, and China. Like Ghana and Mali, these powerful city-states were governed by kings who converted to Islam, ruled as caliphs, and taxed the trade. They built stone mosques and public buildings and dressed in silk from China. In the 1200s, the kingdom of **Zimbabwe** created a magnificent stone complex known as Great Zimbabwe, which was a city of stone towers, palaces, and public buildings.

❷ EUROPE DURING THE HIGH MIDDLE AGES (around 1000 to 1450 CE)

While the traditional feudal economy was based on agriculture in the countryside, a new premodern economy was evolving by the year 1100 CE. After centuries of decline, increased trade began to stimulate the growth of commercial cities. Most often located on riversides, these towns grew into marketplaces where goods could be sold. Located in Flanders, **Bruges** was ideally located on a river system that connected the North Sea with Central Europe along the Rhine. Cross-channel trade brought raw wool from England, which was made into clothing to sell. Part of a league of cities called the Hanseatic League, **Hamburg** was a major port on the North Sea. The League regulated taxes and created rules for fair trade among the member cities. Also, the central Italian city of **Florence** controlled the flow of goods up and down the peninsula. This city-state became a center for banking and commerce by 1300 CE. Among those providing services were barbers, blacksmiths, coopers (barrel makers), jewelers, leatherworkers (tanners), innkeepers, and wine/beer merchants. These cities began to plan their growth, regulate business, and collect taxes.

Crusades (1095 to 1204 CE)

The Crusades were a series of Christian holy wars conducted against "infidels." The most significant was a massive expedition led by the Roman Catholic Church to recapture Palestine (the land of Christian origins) from the Muslims. **Pope Urban II** launched the Crusades in 1095 CE, when he called for Christian knights to take up arms and seize the Holy Land.

After the First Crusade, the Christians captured Edessa, Antioch, and Jerusalem and carved up that territory into feudal states, but the disorganized Muslim forces reorganized and retook Jerusalem in 1187 CE. The Fourth Crusade never made it to the Holy Land. The crusaders, aided by the merchants of Venice, conquered and sacked Constantinople, the capital of the Byzantine Empire. Thus the crusaders had stopped fighting Muslims and had begun fighting Christians. They held the city for over 50 years until it was retaken. Though the quest for the Holy Land was a failure, it led to great economic developments in Europe; it encouraged **trade with Muslim merchants** and created an increase in European demand for Asian goods. As a result, Italian merchants from places like Venice and Genoa greatly profited, and Europe was reintroduced to the goods, technology, and culture of the outside world.

The period 600 to 1450 CE witnessed a large increase in the volume of long-distance trade. Overland trade included luxury goods of high value, such as silk and precious stones. The sea lanes were used for transporting bulkier commodities such as steel, stone, coral, and building materials.

❯❯ MISSIONARY CAMPAIGNS

Buddhism

Theravada Buddhism, the stricter form of the religion, spread to Southeast Asia, while **Mahayana** Buddhism spread to Central and East Asia. The latter form focused more on meditation and on rituals and included the worship of holy people, known as bodhisattvas. Along the Silk Road, Buddhism traveled to **Central Asia** and adapted to polytheism. In **Tibet,** Buddhism became popular as it combined shamanism and the importance of rituals. In East Asia, monks, merchants, and missionaries adapted Buddhism to the political ideas of Confucianism by including ancestor worship and a focus on family, mixing in Daoist ideas. Chinese Buddhism spread to **Korea,** where it received royal support, and to **Japan.** In Japan, it was initially resisted by Shinto leaders, but eventually, **syncretism** (the fusion of differing systems of beliefs) occurred as Buddhism incorporated the worship of Shinto divinities.

Christianity

While the Western Roman Empire was declining, Christian missionary efforts turned toward Northern Europe. The Western Church and the **Pope** sponsored missionary campaigns aimed at converting the Germanic people. The Eastern Orthodox Church also spread Christianity to Eastern Europe and Russia. As with Buddhism, syncretism aided the spread of Christianity. Pagan heroes or holy figures (the saints) were seen as mediators between God and his people. Polytheistic holidays such as winter solstice were incorporated by placing Christmas on the same day. In Asia, **Nestorian Christianity** spread to Mesopotamia and Persia, where Islamic conquerors allowed Christians to practice their religion. Merchants spread Nestorian Christianity as far as India, Central Asia, and China, but they received little support from the established rulers.

Islam

Islam spread through two main avenues: **military conquest,** and **trade and missionary activity.** Through military conquest and political influence, the religion spread because of its **tolerance** for other beliefs (people were rarely forced to convert) and a special tax levied against non-Muslims. Through trade and missionary activity, the religion spread because of its simple message of what to do and what not to do. Plus, lower-class individuals welcomed their inclusion as spiritual equals as well as Islam's emphasis on charity.

Islam also legitimized the role of merchants. The **Sufis** were the most active missionaries after 900 CE, spreading Islam to Southern Europe, sub-Saharan Africa, Central Asia, India, and Southeast Asia. In sub-Saharan Africa, merchants introduced Islam to the ruling class through trade, where syncretism occurred. The kings still held a divine position, and women continued to have a prominent place in society, as was the local custom. In East Africa, Islam arrived via the Indian Ocean. In India, Turks brought Islam in the 11th century when they formed the Delhi Sultanate; they told Hindu stories with Muslim characters, attracting both warriors and low-caste Hindus.

❯❯ TRAVELERS: IBN BATTUTA, MARCO POLO, AND RABBAN SAUMA

The tremendous amount of long-distance interaction in this period can be illustrated through the travels of three individuals. **Ibn Battuta** (1304–1369 CE) was a Muslim scholar from Morocco who traveled throughout Dar al-Islam: West Africa, India, Southeast Asia. He demonstrated the widespread influence of Islam and found a government position as a **qadi** or judge in the lands in which he traveled. **Marco Polo** (1254–1324 CE) was an Italian merchant from Venice who traveled over the Silk Road to the Mongolian Empire in China, where he was allowed by Kublai Khan to pursue mercantile and domestic missions. **Rabban Sauma** (1220–1294 CE) was a Nestorian Christian priest from the Mongolian Empire who began a pilgrimage to Jerusalem. He started in Beijing, but was diverted when he was sent by the Mongol Ilkhanate of Persia to meet with kings of France and England and the Pope to negotiate alliances against Muslims.

❯❯ THE SPREAD OF DISEASE: PLAGUE (1340s to late 1600s CE)

Along with the spread of religion, technology, and goods along the trade routes came disease. The **Black Plague** spread from the Yunnan region of southwest China by way of rodents. In the 1340s, Mongols, merchants, and travelers spread the disease even farther along the trade routes west of China. Oasis towns, trading cities of Central Asia, Black Sea ports, the Mediterranean Sea, and Western Europe were all affected. Most victims of this devastating disease died in just a few days. As a result, the population decreased significantly, causing great **labor shortages**. In Western Europe, workers demanded higher wages and peasants rebelled, leading to a decrease in serfdom and a weakening of the feudal system. **Anti-Semitism** also increased as Jews, used as scapegoats, were accused of poisoning the wells.

❯❯ RENAISSANCE BEGINNINGS IN ASIA AND EUROPE (1400 CE)

Chinese Development

In 1368, Emperor Hongwu started the **Ming dynasty** following the collapse of the Mongol-led Yuan dynasty. The Confucian education system and civil service exam were reinstated. The Ming relied on **mandarins**, a class of powerful officials, to implement their policies. Laborers rebuilt irrigation systems, and agricultural production increased. Private merchants traded porcelain, silk, and cotton, and the navy was refurbished. From 1405 to 1433, seven massive naval expeditions were sponsored to re-establish Chinese presence in the Indian Ocean. Projects were funded that emphasized Chinese cultural traditions, such as the **Yongle Encyclopedia** and printing. **Jesuit missionaries** such as Matteo Ricci arrived, introducing European technology. The Ming dynasty lasted until 1644 CE.

European Development

Strong, powerful **monarchies**, like those in Milan, Venice, and Florence, were now in a position to tax citizens directly and to maintain large standing armies. In Spain, Fernando of Aragon married Isabella of Castille and the combined armies of their powerful kingdoms united Spain by reconquering the lands formerly controlled by Muslims. The **competition** seen among these states led to a refinement in weapons, ships, and technology, and the movement known as the **Renaissance** began. Contact with the **Islamic world** reintroduced ancient Greek and Roman texts that had been preserved by Arabs. In the 1300s–1500s, artists drew inspiration from the **Greek** and **Roman** classical past, and

Leonardo da Vinci and **Michelangelo** used perspective to create realistic works of art. Noble families like the **Medicis** had grown wealthy as merchants, and the **Portuguese** were the early leaders in exploration, setting up sailing schools and sponsoring expeditions along the West African coast.

Native American Empires

MAYA (around 300 to 900 CE)

Borrowing from earlier Olmec traditions, the Mayans controlled a large domain and lived in scattered settlements on the Yucatan peninsula in southern Mexico. Mayans developed an agricultural economy (based on corn and beans), massive pyramids, ritualistic polytheism, and trade-oriented city-states.

AZTEC (around 1400 to 1521 CE)

Also known as the Mexica people, the Aztecs were the last great Mesoamerican culture before the arrival of the Europeans. Taking advantage of the Toltecs' decline, the Aztecs used their fighting skills to take control of the Lake Texcoco region in central Mexico. The Aztec culture was characterized by a militant warrior tradition, rule by severe despots, and priests who conducted many rituals, including human sacrifice. Aztec culture featured a polytheistic religion with an extensive pantheon and a large urban capital with 150,000 inhabitants who lived off an agricultural economy with cacao beans sometimes used as currency.

INCA (around 1300 to 1540 CE)

In the 1300s CE, the Incan clans conquered a large area and absorbed many tribes in central-western South America. In 90 years, the Incan Empire grew to cover over 3,000 miles from north to south. The Incas had their capital at Cuzco (in present-day Peru), which featured an extensive, irrigated agricultural system that was adapted to the rugged terrain of the Andes. The Incans had a polytheistic religion centered on worship of the sun, but they had no written language, despite their impressive achievements in building with cut stone. They did, however, develop a complex record keeping system using *quipu*, knotted, colored strings used to maintain official records.

> ### ▷ AP EXPERT TIP
>
> Migrations are an important part of world history, even today. Knowing why peoples move (political, economic, cultural, or environmental reasons called push–pull factors) and the consequences of their movements is an essential element in understanding the development of human civilization during this time frame. You should be able to compare the causes and effects of the migrations of the Vikings, Turks, Mongols, Aztecs, and Arabs.

Practice Section

❯❯ DOCUMENT-BASED QUESTION

This DBQ is a practice activity. The actual question on the exam will have 6 to 10 documents.

Directions: The following question is based on the accompanying Documents 1 to 4. This question is designed to test your ability to work with and understand historical documents and write an essay that:

- Has a relevant thesis and supports that thesis with evidence from the documents
- Uses all of the documents
- Analyzes the documents by grouping them in as many appropriate ways as possible; **does not simply summarize the documents individually**
- Takes into account the sources of the documents and analyzes the authors' points of view
- Explains the need for at least one additional type of document

You may refer to relevant historical information not mentioned in the documents. Based on the following documents, analyze and discuss the motivations for the Crusades. Explain what additional type of document(s) would help assess the motivations for the Crusades.

Document 1

Source: Pope Leo IV (847–855 CE): Forgiveness of Sins for Those Who Die in Battle with the Heathen

Given to the Frankish Army: "Now we hope that none of you will be slain, but we wish you to know that the kingdom of heaven will be given as a reward to those who shall be killed in this war. For the Omnipotent knows that they lost their lives fighting for the truth of the faith, for the preservation of their country, to aid the defense of Christians. And therefore God will give them the reward which we have named."

Document 2

Source: Pope John VIII: Indulgence for Fighting the Heathen, 878 CE

Directed to the bishops in the realm of Louis II [the Stammerer]: "You have modestly expressed a desire to know whether those who have recently died in war, fighting in defense of the church of God and for the preservation of the Christian religion and of the state, or those who may in the future fall in the same cause, may obtain indulgence for their sins. We confidently reply that those who, out of love to the Christian religion, shall die in battle fighting bravely against pagans or unbelievers shall receive eternal life. For the Lord has said through his prophet: 'In whatever hour a sinner shall be converted, I will remember his sins no longer.' By the intercession of St. Peter, who has the power of binding and loosing in heaven and on the earth, we absolve, as far as is permissible, all such and commend them by our prayers to the Lord."

Document 3

Source: Pope Gregory VII: Call for a Crusade, 1074 CE

Greeting and apostolic benediction: "We hereby inform you that the bearer of this letter, on his recent return from across the sea [from Palestine], came to Rome to visit us. He repeated what we had heard from many others, that a pagan race had overcome the Christians and with horrible cruelty had devastated everything almost to the walls of Constantinople, and were now governing the conquered lands with tyrannical violence, and that they had slain many thousands of Christians as if they were but sheep. If we love God and wish to be recognized as Christians, we should be filled with grief at the misfortune of this great empire [the Greek] and the murder of so many Christians. But simply to grieve is not our whole duty. The example of our Redeemer and the bond of fraternal love demand that we should lay down our lives to liberate them. 'Because he has laid down his life for us: and we ought to lay down our lives for the brethren,' [1 John 3:16]. Know, therefore, that we are trusting in the mercy of God and in the power of his might and that we are striving in all possible ways and making preparations to render aid to the Christian Empire [the Greek] as quickly as possible. Therefore we beseech you by the faith in which you are united through Christ in the adoption of the sons of God, and by the authority of St. Peter, prince of apostles, we admonish you that you be moved to proper compassion by the wounds and blood of your brethren and the danger of the aforesaid empire and that, for the sake of Christ, you undertake the difficult task of bearing aid to your brethren [the Greeks]. Send messengers to us at once to inform us of what God may inspire you to do in this matter."

Document 4

Source: Chronicle of Fulcher of Chartres, written between 1101 and 1128 CE

Fulcher was present at the Council of Clermont, where Pope Urban II issued his call for the First Crusade in 1095 and participated in the Crusades.

The Pope's Exhortation Concerning the Expedition to Jerusalem:

3. "For, as most of you have been told, the Turks, a race of Persians, who have penetrated within the boundaries of Romania even to the Mediterranean to that point which they call the Arm of Saint George, in occupying more and more of the lands of the Christians, have overcome them, already victims of seven battles, and have killed and captured them, have overthrown churches, and have laid waste God's kingdom. If you permit this supinely for very long, God's faithful ones will be still further subjected.

4. "Concerning this affair, I, with suppliant prayer—not I but the Lord, exhort you, heralds of Christ, to persuade all of whatever class, both knights and footman, both rich and poor, in numerous edicts, to strive to help expel that wicked race from our Christian lands before it is too late.

5. "I speak to those present, I send word to those not here; moreover, Christ commands it. Remission of sins will be granted for those going thither, if they end a shackled life either on land or in crossing the sea, or in struggling against the heathen. I, being vested with that gift from God, grant this to those who go."

❯ HOW TO APPROACH THE DOCUMENT-BASED QUESTION

The first of the three essays is the document-based question (DBQ). This essay **asks you to be a historian**; it will ask a specific question, provide a bit of historical background, and then present 6–10 related documents. Essentially, you are the historian who will take these sources and draw conclusions based on your skills of historical analysis. The DBQ evaluates historical understanding at its purest: The task is not to remember facts but to organize information in an analytical manner. Many students panic once they see the DBQ because they do not know much about the topic—the question and the documents often cover something well outside of the mainstream of high school classes. The test writers do this on purpose. Outside knowledge is not needed for the DBQ. You may bring in outside information if you wish, but there is no need to mention facts other than those found in the documents provided. (This approach is different than the DBQ task on the AP U.S. History exam.)

The other two essays on the exam will evaluate your knowledge of history, but the DBQ evaluates your proficiency with historical material. Consequently, writing the DBQ is a skill that can be learned much like any other skill.

Organizing Your Essay in 10 Minutes

The entire 130-minute essay time is divided into two parts: The first 10 minutes is reading and organizing time, during which you may not write in the pink essay booklet, and the last 120 minutes is the essay-writing period when you will write all three essays. Spend that first 10 minutes working solidly on the DBQ, since that is the essay that requires the most reading and preparation time.

Feel free to write notes in the green question booklet as you read the documents. Nothing in the green booklet is read as part of the essay scoring. Feel free to underline important words in both the source line and the document itself. Use the generous margins for notes that will help you group the documents with other documents and discuss their points of view.

While taking notes, write the following about the authors of the document in the margins: social class, education, occupation, and gender. On the bottom of the document, write a short phrase that summarizes the basic meaning of the document, the purpose (why it was written), and, possibly, a missing piece of evidence that relates to the document. If the document is a speech, the missing evidence could be the perception of those listening to the speech. If the document is a government declaration, the missing evidence could be information about how effectively the declaration was carried out. It is also helpful to pause after reading all of the documents to consider evidence that would provide a more complete understanding of the issue. Then suggest an additional document.

Once you have finished reading and have made short notes of all of the documents, reread the question. Note again what the question asks. If you have not done so already, mark which documents address the different issues that the question asks. Group the documents by their similarities. Can you draw enough conclusions at this point to organize an analytical thesis?

Core Point Scoring

For fairness and ease of scoring, the essays for AP World History are evaluated using what is called a "core scoring method" that comes from scoring rubrics. Each essay is scored on a 10-point system from 0 to 9, with 9 being the best. With the DBQ, the first 7 points are awarded for the completion of specific tasks. These are called the "basic core" points. Up to an extra 2 points ("expanded core" points) may be awarded after all of the essential core points are met. For the DBQ, the basic core points are as follows:

POINTS TASK

1   Has an acceptable thesis.

1   Understands the basic meaning of documents (may misinterpret one document).

2   Supports thesis with appropriate evidence from all or all but one of the documents.

   (1)   Supports thesis with appropriate evidence from all but two documents.

1   Analyzes point of view in at least two documents.

1   Analyzes documents by grouping them in three ways.

1   Identifies and explains the need for one type of appropriate additional document or source.

7   *Subtotal for all basic core points*

2   Possible expanded core points (for excellence)

9   *Total possible points for the DBQ*

Final Notes on How to Write the DBQ

DO:

- Take notes in the margins during the reading period relating to the background of the speaker and his or her possible point of view.
- Assume that each document provides only a snapshot of the topic—just one perspective.
- Look for connections between documents for grouping.
- Mark off documents that you use in the green booklet so that you do not forget to mention them.
- Refer to the authorship of the documents as you are writing, not just the document numbers.
- Mention additional documents and the reasons why they would help one further analyze the question.
- Mark off each part of the instructions for the essay as you accomplish them.

DON'T:

- Repeat information from the historical background in your essay.
- Assume that the documents are universally valid rather than offering single perspectives.
- Avoid visual and graphic information in those kinds of documents.
- Spend too much time on the DBQ rather than moving on to the other two essays.
- Write the first paragraph before you have a clear idea of what your thesis will be.
- Ignore part of the question.
- Structure the essay with just one paragraph.
- Write in the present tense.
- Underline or highlight the thesis (this may be done as an exercise for class, but on the test it looks juvenile).

❯❯ DOCUMENT-BASED QUESTION: SAMPLE RESPONSE

From 600 to 1450 CE, the Catholic Church established much authority over the Western European world. Kings during this period were relatively ineffectual, and the Pope was the centralizing figure in the region. As the Islamic culture became more dominant and powerful, the Catholic Church noticed and felt threatened. In an effort to combat the Muslim threat, the Church called for a series of Crusades. The purpose of these crusades was to limit the Muslims, ideologically and geographically, and to protect fellow Christians. The inspiration given to employ willing participants in these journeys to the East was mainly religious and political.

Because the Catholic Church held the authority to choose who could receive salvation, a major religious motivation for participation in the Crusades was the guarantee of eternal life. Pope Leo IV, with the intention of motivating the troops, gave a message to the Frankish army in the ninth century that promised heaven as the repayment for anyone who was killed in battle. Since the Franks, according to the Pope, were fighting for the truth of the faith and helping to defend Christians, God would nurture them in the afterlife. Later in the ninth century, Pope John VIII gave a message to his bishops, again with the purpose of motivating and encouraging participation in the fight. This message promised indulgence (forgiveness) for the sins of those who fought for the Christian religion and state. It would be helpful to know if the bishops receiving the pope's letter were convinced of the validity of this mission and, more importantly, if the soldiers who received the promise of salvation were truly motivated by this reason or other more economic reasons, such as the chance to obtain their own land. Lastly, Pope Urban II, as told by Fulcher of Chartres, informed his listeners at the Council of Clermont in 1095 CE that Christ commanded the Crusades and that those who participated would have their sins automatically absolved. Pope Urban, also, with the intent to stir up hatred for the Muslim people, told his audience that the Muslims had already killed and captured Christians and had destroyed God's churches in the name of their own, supposedly infidel, god.

In addition to the religious reasons to participate in the Crusades, the Church used political incentives to persuade people to participate. In his letter, Pope John VIII openly associated Christianity and the state, giving the mission a political, as well as religious, function. By doing this, the Pope made the government an instrument of the Church. Almost 200 years later, in 1074 CE, Pope Gregory VII called for his own Crusade. In his statement, he pointed out that "a pagan race had overcome Christians and with horrible cruelty had devastated everything almost to the walls of Constantinople, and were now governing the conquered lands with tyrannical violence...." His intention was to compare the Muslims to an almost subhuman race that was threatening Christian civilization. His was attempting to appeal to Western European Christians to defend their fellow Christians in the Byzantine Empire, thus inciting a religious and political bond between the two. Since the call from Pope Urban II in 1095 initiated the Crusades to recapture the Holy land in Palestine, it would be helpful to know how Pope Gregory's message was received and why the mass movement did not begin after his call for a Crusade. Additionally, did the average Christian in Western Europe feel a loyalty to Byzantine Christians because of their common faith, or were there other reasons to get involved, as in monetary gain or an increase in social status?

After Pope Urban's effort to mobilize a Crusade in 1095 CE, the next 200 years involved a movement by the Catholic Church and Christian kingdoms to reconquer the Holy Land. The Church used both religious motivation (the promise of salvation) and political motivation (the reconquering of land) to stir up involvement. Additionally, the economic motive of potential wealth and land drove many crusaders into the Crusade movement, regardless of outcome.

CHAPTER 3

The First Global Age (1450 to 1750 CE)

❯❯ A THUMBNAIL VIEW

- As a result of the search for a faster way to the trade routes of the Indian Ocean, the Americas were included in the global trade network, and the process of true globalization began. The European nations gained access to Asian trade routes and attempted to control them. Interaction between Europeans and Native Americans set off the Colombian Exchange of goods, disease, and cultures, which spread throughout the world.

- Improvements in and the spread of shipping technologies and gunpowder weapons allowed European countries to begin to exercise a more prominent role in world affairs.

❯ AP EXPERT TIP

Create a list of key terms like *nation-state* and even common words like *commerce* and quiz fellow classmates on their meaning. This is not an exam you can cram for. There is literally too much information. Start reviewing early—at least six weeks out. A glossary of some key terms appears in the back of this book.

- Native American people died by the millions due to their exposure to previously unknown European diseases. African people were forcibly transported across the Atlantic Ocean to fill the need for forced labor on plantations.

- New social structures emerged like those in the Americas based on race. Those with pure European blood were considered the highest status socially and politically, and those with Native American or African blood were considered the lowest. While few women exerted power publicly, women of the harem in the Ottoman Empire wielded considerable power behind the scenes.

- In Europe, the Renaissance and Reformation challenged previously accepted beliefs and the power of the Roman Catholic Church. In other parts of the world, such as China, reaffirmation of more traditional beliefs was viewed as the key to stability.

- European Empires such as Spain and Portugal stretched their power overseas to conquer and control the newly encountered Americas. At the same time, dominant land-based empires such as the Ottoman, Mughal, and Qing grew powerful.

❯ IMPACT OF COMMUNICATION—GROWTH OF A WORLD ECONOMY

European Exploration

As discussed in the last chapter, the Ming dynasty had extensively explored the Indian Ocean from 1405 to 1433 CE, but under pressure from conservative forces, it decided to halt the voyages and destroy the ships. The Indian Ocean continued to be a thriving trade route, however, with participants such as **Arabs, Indians, Malays,** and others. So when the European powers entered Indian Ocean trade, they were not so much creating this vibrant trade route as inserting themselves into an existing one. But when they did so, the world shifted from a primarily Asian-centered economy to a global economy.

As Europe emerged from its more isolated and self-sufficient period, the desire to explore came with it. The major motivations for this exploration included the search for resources and for new trade routes to Asian markets and the desire to spread Christianity. The Asian goods that Europe received such as **pepper, ginger, cloves,** and **nutmeg** were very expensive. Europeans wanted to gain direct access to these trade items and cut out the middleman who controlled overland trade routes between Asia and Europe. Additionally, **the Ottoman conquest of Constantinople in 1453** destroyed the last vestiges of the Byzantine Empire, solidifying Muslim influence in the region and making it less friendly to European traders. The acquisition of technology from China and the Muslim world helped the Europeans expand their seagoing capabilities with such innovations as the sternpost rudder, triangular lateen sails, magnetic compass, and astrolabe. The early leader in exploration was Portugal, which established sugar plantations on islands in the Atlantic off the coast of Africa, but many other expeditions would follow.

Explorers and Accomplishments

- **Bartolomeu Dias (Portugal) in 1488:** Rounded Cape of Good Hope at the tip of Africa and entered the Indian Ocean.
- **Christopher Columbus (Spain) in 1492:** Sailed west to reach Asia and instead reached the Bahamas. Sailed around Caribbean.
- **Vasco de Gama (Spain) in 1497:** Reached Calicut in India by rounding Africa.
- **Magellan (Spain) in 1519–1522:** Sailed around South America to the Philippine Islands (where he was killed); his men sailed back through the Indian Ocean and were the first to circumnavigate the globe.

TRADING-POST EMPIRES

The initial goal of European powers in exploring the Indian Ocean was not to conquer but rather to control the lucrative trade. They wanted to force merchant ships to trade in fortified trading sites and to pay duties for the privilege. By the mid-1500s, Portugal had 50 trading posts from West Africa to East Asia, but by the late 1500s, its power began to decline. This small country with its small population could not sustain a large seaborne empire.

The English and the Dutch quickly took Portugal's place as the dominant powers with their faster, cheaper, and more powerful ships. Additionally, they used **joint stock companies,** in which investors rather than the crown funded the expeditions.

COLOMBIAN EXCHANGE

The inclusion of the Americas in the global trade network, following the voyages of Columbus, set off the global diffusion of plants, food, crops, animals, humans, and diseases known as the Colombian Exchange. The most devastating effect of this diffusion was the spread of **smallpox** to the Americas, to which the native people had no immunity. The Aztec Empire lost 95 percent of its population within a century and, in this weakened state, was controlled by its Spanish conquerors. Between 1500 and 1800, 100 million people died from the spread of disease to the Americas. The **diffusion of food crops and animals** also revolutionized life around the world, leading to an increase in the nutritional value of diets and a population increase worldwide.

ROLE AND IMPACT OF SILVER

Silver, the most abundant American precious metal, was responsible for stimulating a truly global trade network. The two areas rich in silver were Mexico and the Potosi mines in the Andes, which employed large numbers of Native American laborers (often forced). Driven by China's desire for silver, this mining industry powered the Spanish economy and stimulated the world economy. It was used to trade for silk and porcelain in Asia, and it financed Spain's powerful army and bureaucracy; in order for the Spanish to purchase Chinese goods at that time, they needed to use American silver.

ROLE AND IMPACT OF SUGAR

Another influential product of this time period was sugar. The cultivation and production of sugar involved a complex use of land, labor, buildings, animals, capital, and technical skills. It required both heavy labor (for planting and harvesting the cane) and specialized skills (for the sugar-making process). Because smallpox had wiped out so many native peoples in the Americas, enslaved Africans became the main labor force. These slaves worked under very harsh conditions—mistreatment, extreme heat, and poor nutrition—leading to significant disease and death. These sugar plantations were, in all aspects, proto-factories in that they were financed and organized to create a single product in a complex manufacturing process that took place in one area (resembling the future manufacturing processes of the Industrial Revolution). Certainly the lessons learned from the sugar plantations would be assimilated by generations of European businessmen and eventually translated into the textile industry, thus kicking off the Industrial Revolution of the 19th century.

Traveling Goods
Europe to the Americas
Wheat
Sugarcane
Cotton
Horses
Cattle
Pigs
Sheep
Goats
Chickens
The Americas to Africa, Asia, and Europe
Maize
Potatoes
Beans
Tomatoes
Peppers
Peanuts
Avocadoes
Pineapples
Tobacco

❯❯ THE DEVELOPMENT OF STATES

Ottoman Empire (early 1300s to 1923)

The Ottoman Empire got its start as a band of seminomadic Turks who migrated to northwest Anatolia in the 13th century, but through military might and gunpowder weapons, it turned into a major political power. An elite fighting force of slave troops made of Christian boys (called **janissaries**) led the military. In 1453 CE, the Ottomans captured Constantinople and named it Istanbul. Under the leadership of sultans such as **Mehmed** and **Suleyman**, a centralized absolute monarchy ruled. In the capital city Istanbul, the cathedral **Hagia Sophia** was converted to a grand mosque. The sultan's concubines and female relatives resided in the harem and wielded political power. Concubines, who were often slaves, were educated in reading, the Koran, sewing, and music, and played a significant role in state politics. The sultan's mother, who was given the title Queen Mother, exercised considerable power as an advisor to the throne. The empire reached its peak in the mid-1600s, but as European military and naval technology outpaced theirs, the Ottomans were ill equipped to compete. The Ottoman empire continued to exist until it was finally broken apart after World War I.

Mughal India (1523 to mid-1700s)

India was conquered by Babur, who established the Mughal Empire. Babur, a descendant of Turkic nomads, began his conquest of India in 1526, and his grandson **Akbar** created a religion called the Divine Faith in which he combined elements of Islam and Hinduism to promote religious unity. He encouraged intermarriage, he **abolished the jizya** (non-Muslim tax), and he promoted Hindus to high-ranking government jobs. His descendants, Jahangir and Shah Jahan, were also **great patrons of the arts.** Mughal architecture often blended Persian and Hindu traditions by using Islamic domes, arches, and minarets, along with Hindu ornamentation. The most famous example of Mughal architecture is the **Taj Mahal.** Shah Jahan's son seized the throne and pushed to extend Muslim control to all of India. He also sought to rid India of Hindu influences (bringing back the non-Muslim tax), and his many wars drained the treasury. Peasant uprisings and revolts by both Muslim and Hindu princes weakened the empire.

Songhay (1464 to 1591)

In the 1400s, the West African state of Songhay emerged to take power over the weakened Mali Empire. Its leader, Sunni Ali, consolidated his empire by appointing governors to oversee the provinces, building a hierarchically commanded army, and creating an imperial navy to patrol the Niger River. The lucrative **trans-Saharan trade** flowed through the city of Gao, which brought salt, textiles, and metal in exchange for gold and slaves. After Sunni Ali, all Songhay emperors were **Muslims** who supported mosques, schools, and the Islamic university at **Timbuktu.** As Europeans began making inroads into Africa, the Songhay Empire began to lose control; the empire went into decline and was defeated by the Moroccans in 1591.

Kongo (around 1300s to 1600s)

In the 14th century, the Kongo emerged as a **centralized state** along the west coast of central Africa. In 1482, a small **Portuguese** fleet arrived and initiated **commercial relations,** and within a few years the Portuguese had developed a close political and diplomatic relationship with the king. The king converted to **Christianity** in an effort to improve commercial and diplomatic relations. The interaction brought wealth and foreign recognition to Kongo, but it eventually led to its decline. The Portuguese brought textiles, weapons, and craftsmen there, and they wanted gold, silver, and ivory. They especially wanted slaves, though, and in exchange for weapons, they began **slave raids** with the cooperation of local leaders. These dealings undermined the king's authority, and Kongo was defeated in war with the Portuguese in 1665.

Spanish and Portuguese Overseas Expansion/Empire (1500s to early 1800s)

Although Spanish conquistadors led the way in the conquest of the Americas, the Spanish crown was not far behind. The two major areas of the empire—New Spain (Mexico) and New Castile (Peru)—were each governed by a **viceroy,** who was responsible to the Spanish king. In 1494, the Treaty of Tordesillas divided the Americas in half: the Spanish controlled the west, and the Portuguese controlled the east. The social result of the conquest of the Americas was a multicultural and ethnically mixed population. The **peninsulares,** the highest social class, came directly from the Iberian Peninsula, and their descendants were the **Creoles.** The mix of Europeans and Native Americans were the **mestizos,** and the mix of European and Africans were the **mulattoes.** At the bottom of the social order were the Native Americans, Africans, and the mixed class of **zambos.** Economically, the empire thrived with silver mining, farming, stock raising, and craft production. Right behind the conquistadors came the **missionaries,** who hoped to spread Christianity.

Qing Dynasty (1644 to 1911)

A nomadic people from lands to the north east of China, the **Manchu**, took over as the Qing dynasty. China thus came under the rule of foreigners for the second time. The Manchu had made a conscious effort to mimic Chinese culture generations before this and, unlike the Mongols, bolstered many aspects of Chinese government, including using the Confucian civil service exam system. Like the Mongols, however, the Manchu wanted to preserve their own ethnic and cultural identity, so they forbade intermarriage between Manchu and Han Chinese and forbade the Chinese from traveling to Manchuria and from learning their Manchu language.

Russian Empire (1480 to 1917)

Ivan III, a grand prince of Moscow, stopped paying tribute to the Mongols and, in 1480, began building an empire for himself. He established a strong central government ruled by an absolute monarch, the **czar,** who was also the head of the **Russian Orthodox Church.** The czar received his authority from God. After a reign of terror by Ivan the Terrible, the **Romanov family** came to power, and it ruled Russia for the next 300 years. **Peter the Great,** who reigned from 1682 to 1725, was fascinated with **Western technology** and instituted a policy of forced and rapid modernization. He constructed the capital city, **St. Petersburg,** as his window to the West.

Japan: Tokugawa Shogunate (1603 to 1867)

After a period of civil war and disorder, **Tokugawa Leyasu** established the Tokugawa Shogunate in 1603. He increased his control over the **daimyos,** insisting that they spend every other year at the **capital, Edo (now Tokyo).** Japanese were forbidden from going abroad and from constructing large ships. Europeans were expelled from Japan, and foreign merchants were not allowed to trade in Japanese ports (the only exception was a small number of Chinese and Dutch ships). Despite all these restrictions, the Japanese **economy grew,** as agricultural production increased and the samurai became government administrators. Christianity had made some important inroads in Japan by 1580, with 150,000 Japanese Christian converts, but the government ended these missions. The **Dutch merchants** continued to be the principal source of information about Europe.

❯ ORGANIZATION OF SLAVERY AND INDENTURED SERVITUDE

Atlantic Slave Trade

The forced migration of over 15 million Africans to the New World was one of the most significant outcomes of both the Age of Exploration and the Columbian Exchange that followed. Slavery had existed in Africa since ancient times: tribes would often take prisoners from neighboring tribes and enslave them. African law did not recognize private property, so land did not equal wealth. Control over human labor was what equaled wealth. The spread of Islam also established new trade routes across the northern part of the continent that took enslaved Africans to the Middle East.

By the time Europeans ventured into sub-Saharan Africa, the slave traffic had been well established for 500 years. The Portuguese explored the west coast of Africa in the 1500s, establishing trade relations with various tribes, and after they secured a piece of the New World in Brazil, they brought slaves from Africa for their newly established **plantations.** The slave trade had become **transoceanic,** and profits from it encouraged other Europeans to enter the business.

By the mid-1600s, competing stations and fleets brought thousands of enslaved Africans monthly across the ocean. This ocean journey, known as the **Middle Passage,** consisted of a four- to six-week trip below decks in cramped quarters. The death toll en route was considerable, and many Africans died upon arrival at the tropical fields of South

America. For most African slaves, the end destinations were either Brazil or the sugar plantations in the Caribbean. The **triangular trade** that developed sent European manufactured goods (firearms, in particular) to Africa for slaves, slaves to the Caribbean and American mainland, and American products back to Europe.

As more enslaved people were brought to the coast, African kingdoms reoriented their economies to trade with the Europeans. Some African societies benefited economically from the trade, but several experienced severe population loss. Also, many slaves were traded for guns, and the addition of firearms led to an increase in political conflict in Africa.

Plantation societies were located in the most tropical regions of the Americas, cultivating **cash crops** such as sugar, tobacco, cotton, or coffee. The goal of the plantation was to gain as much profit as possible from the export of these cash crops. Though many of the enslaved Africans were Christianized by the Europeans, they retained parts of their language and culture. A unique cultural synthesis occurred as African music, dress, and mannerisms mixed with Spanish and indigenous cultures in the Americas.

Encomienda System

The early Spanish settlers in the Americas and the Caribbean needed to recruit a great deal of labor. In fact, the **encomienda system** gave them the **right to demand labor** in the mines and fields from native peoples. The laborers were worked hard and punished severely. Cortez and Pizarro brought this system to the American mainland. On the **haciendas** (large estates), Native Americans were often abused; as a result, Spanish officials replaced the encomienda system with the **repartimiento system**. This system compelled Native American communities **to supply labor** for Spanish mines and farms, but it limited their work time and it compensated them with wages. Many communities, however, were required to send groups of laborers to work on state projects. In Peru, for instance, the labor system called **mita** mobilized thousands of Native Americans to work in the silver mines. They were paid wages, but there were also many abuses.

Russian Serfdom

After the Mongol rule of Russia, many free peasants fell into **great debt** and were forced to become serfs on large estates. The Russian government encouraged this process beginning in the 1500s because it was a way to satisfy the nobility and to **regulate the peasants** at the same time. As new territories were added to the empire, serfdom extended along with it.

A 1649 act proclaimed that serfs were born into their status and could not escape it. Serfs could be bought and sold, gambled away, and punished by their masters. Whole villages could be sold to supply manufacturing labor. Serfs who were illiterate and poor had to pay high taxes and owed extensive labor service to their landlords in the form of agriculture, mining, or manufacturing.

❯❯ CULTURAL AND INTELLECTUAL CHANGES

European Renaissance (beginning in the 1400s)

Changes and tensions in the 15th century led to new ways of thinking about the nature of humanity and the world. The changes took place slowly, starting on the Italian peninsula. The Crusades had brought Southern Europe into contact with Arab culture, and this stimulated an interest in other cultures and trade. Scholars were uncovering long-forgotten **Roman and Greek** written works that fired the minds of intellectuals. This intellectual reorientation became known as the Renaissance, or "rebirth." The **rebirth** referred to the reappearance of ancient approaches to understanding the world.

Renaissance Italy was a patchwork of feudal domains—lands belonging to the Roman Catholic Church, kingdoms, and city-states. Famous noble families such as the Medicis had grown wealthy as merchants, since Italy was perfectly located for receiving goods from the Middle East and Asia. This lucrative trade with the **Islamic** and **Byzantine cultures** allowed wealthy Italians to become patrons of painters, sculptors, and scientists. The period was also a celebration of the Roman past; classical architecture and engineering were re-examined and relearned.

At the heart of the Renaissance was an intellectual movement called humanism, which focused on worldly subjects rather than on the religious issues that had occupied medieval scholars. Humanists believed that education should stimulate an individual's creative powers.

> ## Hallmarks of the Renaissance
>
> - A new view of man as a creative and rational being
> - A rediscovery of ancient Greco–Roman knowledge
> - Unparalleled accomplishments in literature, music, and art
> - A celebration of the human individual

A new human ideal was created as the concept of a multifaceted **"Renaissance man"** emerged. Perhaps the best example of such a learned and talented individual was **Leonardo da Vinci**. As an artist, scientist, musician, architect, and engineer, he combined the talents of many men into one person.

Protestant Reformation (beginning in the 1500s)

Just as the Renaissance inspired an era of intellectual and artistic exploration, it also created an atmosphere that encouraged debate and criticism of the existing order. The most powerful institution of the day was the Catholic Church, headquartered in Rome. It had held great power over king and peasant alike for centuries and had grown large, wealthy, and corrupt. Practices such as selling forgiveness and salvation began to offend even those in the priesthood.

A movement to reform the Church grew out of these concerns. In 1517, in the German domain of Wittenburg, an obscure priest named **Martin Luther** posted a list of issues that he believed the Church should address. The main issues raised by those who would reform the Church were the following:

- Divisions within the Papacy, in which more than one Pope claimed authority
- Religious traditions and rituals that were not derived from the Scriptures (such as purgatory, pilgrimages, and worship of the saints)
- Corrupt practices such as the sale of indulgences (forgiveness) and religious relics
- Church finances and income
- Lack of piety in the priesthood

Martin Luther's views unleashed a storm of controversy that eventually split the Catholic Church. It also divided Europe between those loyal to the Pope in Rome and those who broke away to form other churches. Luther was excommunicated from the Church but was protected by sympathetic German princes. The German lands were divided among hundreds of small kingdoms, nominally ruled over by the Holy Roman Emperor, in this case Charles V

> ## Outcomes of the Protestant Movement
>
> - A redrawing of the religious map of Europe, with mostly Protestants in the north and Catholics in the south
> - A decline in the power of the Roman Catholic Church
> - Further power struggles between the citizenry and monarchs; in England, when radical Protestants took over the Parliament, civil war erupted and the king was arrested and later publicly beheaded.
> - A series of wars that would pit Catholics and Protestants against each other for the next 200 years

of Spain, a staunch Catholic. Many of the northern German princes resented having to support both an "emperor" who was not German and the Church. Siding with Luther for both religious and political reasons, these princes were called Protestants. The German region was divided into two armed camps, Catholics and Protestants. The resulting **Thirty Years War** (1618–1648) devastated the German lands but ended in a treaty that made each ruler sovereign over his own state and, thus, with the power to choose what religions could be worshiped in his state. The sovereignty of the state became the model for future nation-state relations.

The Protestant movement spread from central Europe to the Netherlands, Switzerland, Scandinavia, France, and Denmark. The English King Henry VIII, once a staunch supporter of the Catholic Church, fell away from the Church after a dispute with the Pope and, with the help of his Parliament, created a new Church of England of which the English monarch was the head.

Enlightenment (beginning in the 1700s)

The Enlightenment is known for its outpouring of **intellectual** and **philosophical thought.** It was centered in France, as that kingdom was the cultural heart of Europe at the time.

Great Thinkers

- **John Locke (England):** Thought all people are born with natural rights and should be free.
- **Voltaire (France):** Said freedom of speech should be permitted.
- **Montesquieu (France):** Urged tolerance and a government segmented into parts that shared power.

A new emphasis on free thought led to the **questioning of traditional authority.** Both the Church and the monarchy were being challenged, and the political radicalism of the Enlightenment would cause great anxiety in the courts of Europe.

As a result of the Roman Catholic mission to China, Jesuits brought back **Chinese knowledge to Europe.** The Confucian civil service exams influenced European rulers, and the rational morality of Confucianism appealed to Enlightenment philosophers.

Scientific Revolution

During the 17th and 18th centuries, a transformation that we call the Scientific Revolution occurred in Europe. This was a logical follow-up to the Renaissance, as more and more people wished to investigate the many mysteries of nature. The Scientific Revolution was primarily a period of intense experimentation and discovery in fields ranging from medicine to engineering.

Part of the revolutionary approach of scientists was the view that the world functions as a machine. Plants, for example, absorb light and release gas, while the human body processes food and turns it into energy. The Scientific Revolution took place over many decades, but it is usually associated with the famous discoveries of people such as Galileo, Francis Bacon, and Isaac Newton.

The Environment

During this time frame, human societies continued to exert mastery over their environment. Perhaps the most significant event was the discovery of the Americas and the resultant Columbian Exchange of crops between the New and

Old Worlds. New foods like the **potato**, which was introduced to Europe from the Americas, had a huge impact on food production and population increases. In the Americas, entire landscapes were stripped to build plantations that grew mostly cash crops like **sugarcane** and **coffee**. This led to a degradation of the topsoil and loss of vegetative cover, thus encouraging flooding and mudslides. The raising of cattle and pigs led to dramatic changes in the landscape; forests were cut for the former, while the latter, with vast feral populations, may have been responsible for the transmission of diseases in the North American regions initially explored by the Spanish. The introduction of horses to the Americas had a significant impact on many Native Americans as they left farming to become nomads, following and hunting the plains-roaming buffalo herds. Of course the most dramatic exchange was that of diseases. Smallpox, measles, and other diseases to which the natives of the Americas had no immunity devastated their populations; some estimates are as high as **90 percent mortality rates**.

The loss of Native Americans played a direct role in their inability to fend off European advancement and also led to the importation of enslaved Africans to work on plantations. Climatically, the Little Ice Age, a several-hundred-year period of cooler temperature, had dramatic impacts on human society. Although no one is in agreement on the exact timing, the period generally lasted from about the late 15th century to the mid-18th century. As temperatures fell, growing seasons shortened, and some types of crops, particularly grains in the north, failed completely. The freezing of rivers and harbors often had dramatic results on warfare, allowing armies to cross what were normally barriers to their movement. At the same time, the harsh conditions took a toll on living conditions in the field, often depleting an army's strength before it could be effective.

A glimmer of awareness of the need to manage natural resources can be seen in the Tokugawa laws in Japan to restrict timbering operations and plant new trees when old ones were cut and in Louis XIV's forestry program to manage France's timber resources. Although these programs were mainly economically motivated, the idea that a nation's resources should be managed by the state would play an important role in the development of future environmental management programs.

Practice Section

CONTINUITY AND CHANGE-OVER-TIME QUESTION

Directions: Answer the following question: You should spend five minutes organizing or outlining your essay. Write an essay that:

- Has a relevant thesis and supports that thesis with appropriate historical evidence
- Addresses all parts of the question
- Substantiates its thesis with appropriate historical evidence
- Analyzes the process of change over time and/or continuity

Choose ONE of the regions below and analyze the changes and continuities in its involvement and roles in **trade** from 600 to 1750 CE.

- *China*
- *Sub-Saharan Africa*
- *South Asia*
- *Middle East*

HOW TO APPROACH THE QUESTION

The continuity and change-over-time (CCOT) question **asks what has changed and what has not.** Here, you must be as detailed as possible with your knowledge of the material. Being good at historical interpretation is not enough; you also need to know history.

Organizing Your Essay in Five Minutes

CCOT questions include a definite time span for analysis. The time span may have the same division dates as the main structural periods for the course: 8000 BCE, 600 CE, 1450 CE, 1750 CE, 1914 CE, and the present. In your green question booklet, you will want to sketch a quick time line and fill in some notes about what happened. Think about breaks in this stretch of time that represented departures from what happened before. Also think about what did *not* change. Start by reading the question, then underline the parts that are most important.

Continuity refers to those aspects that remained the same during the entire stretch of the time period. In this way, it is the *opposite* of the word *change*. The best way to organize your thoughts for the CCOT question is to construct a crude time line in the green question booklet. Remember that the readers do not look at the green booklet when scoring—they look only at the pink answer booklet. Putting together a time line might take a minute or two, but it is helpful.

In your time line notes, you will want to write about social changes that happened. How did gender, family, work, and class structures change? **Do not forget to mention what has stayed the same.** Jot down at least two ideas about continuities throughout this time period.

Core Point Scoring

The CCOT Essay uses a 7-point basic core point system, with an additional expanded core of 2. The 7 points of the basic core are divided among five tasks: two of the tasks count for 2 core points, with a partial credit of 1 point awarded in some instances.

POINTS TASK

1 Has acceptable thesis.

2 Addresses all parts of the question.
   (1) (Addresses most parts of the question.)

2 Substantiates thesis with appropriate historical evidence.
   (1) (Partially substantiates thesis with appropriate historical evidence.)

1 Uses global historical context effectively to explain change over time and/or continuity.

1 Analyzes the process of change over time and/or continuity.

7 *Subtotal for all basic core points*

2 Possible expanded core points (for excellence)

9 *Total possible points for the CCOT*

Do You Have a Thesis?

Your initial task is to present a clear thesis statement. Do not simply restate the question; you must state, instead, the specifics about change and continuity. A strong thesis will deal both with what changed and what stayed the same. Also, in your analysis, be sure to mention the reasons for the changes and continuities.

Do You Go Beyond the Basic Requirements?

Once a CCOT essay has met all 7 basic core points, it is eligible for up to 2 additional points. These points are awarded for excellence above the basic core point standards. Indicators of excellence might include the following:

- A clear and analytical thesis
- An abundance of evidence
- Particularly sophisticated connections to global processes
- Clear chronology with the use of dates associated with events
- Links to a rich variety of events, ideas, and trends
- Deep and even coverage of all parts of the question
- A thorough discussion of continuity in addition to change

Final Notes on How to Write the CCOT

DO:

- Read the question several times so that you understand the tasks required.
- Draw a quick time line in order to organize your thoughts.
- Write a thesis statement that uses the terms of the question while providing analysis.
- Describe in a paragraph the situation at the starting point of the time span.
- Focus on continuities, not just changes.

- Make sure the continuities cover the entire time span of the question.
- Bring in a discussion of the big-picture context of these changes through global processes.
- Mention facts—remember, content is king.

DON'T:
- Discuss events that are not related to the question.
- Include long sections of material outside the time span of the question.
- Focus only on changes and not on continuities.
- Include continuities that apply to only one part of the time span.

❱❱ CONTINUITY AND CHANGE-OVER-TIME QUESTION: SAMPLE RESPONSE

Between 600 and 1750 CE, China was continuously an integral player in the expanding global trade network. However, it simultaneously regressed from being the enthusiastic leader in an expansive world economy to playing more of a supporting role. This transition was partly self-imposed as its worldview and view of itself shifted, though the incorporation of the Americas by Europe into the global economy also caused a decline in China's centrality (even geographic) and dominance. However, while China may have grown more detached from the trade network, it was too strong and influential to ever disassociate completely.

The beginning of these thousand years in history was strong for China. The Tang dynasty was established around the year 600 CE, and it prospered agriculturally (three-field system), politically (civil service examinations), and technologically. These factors combined created a strong, stable China based on a Confucian traditional foundation, allowing for a strong economy to arise. Between 600 and 1450 CE, China was truly the world leader in trade. It increased its presence in and then came to dominate the Indian Ocean and the South China Sea, building connections with the Middle East and Southeast Asia, respectively.

This maritime advancement was made possible by new naval technologies developed under the Tang and Song dynasties, such as the magnetic compass and improved ships. Gunpowder, another technological improvement, would make its way through the trade network to the Middle East and aid the later establishment of Islamic empires and to Europeans, who used firearms to help conquer the Americas. Another change that took place during this earlier period was an increase in industrialization. Especially under Song rule, new port cities were built where Arab and Persian merchants became somewhat assimilated into Chinese society. Larger cities and more expansive trade cycles necessitated the development of new economic systems in China, and paper money, banking, and a "flying cash" system all were established. Also, trade increase leads inevitably to interaction increase, and new religions, such as Buddhism, integrated themselves into Chinese culture. Buddhism blended with the consistently prominent Confucianism to create a new type of Confucianism known as Neo-Confucianism, which had profound political consequences. Throughout this period, China continued using the Silk Road as a means of relations with the Mediterranean world, and Chinese luxury items such as porcelain and silk were in high demand. Closer to the end of this period, the Yuan dynasty (Mongol rule) was replaced by the Chinese Mings, who radically altered China's position as the most dominant global trader.

From around 1450 to 1750, China separated itself from the global market significantly. The beginning of this movement was marked by the closing of many ports and the destruction of ships and travel records by the Ming (though the following Qing dynasty similarly regulated trade). These actions were very consequential, for China lost its dominance in Indian Ocean and Pacific trade, allowing Arabs, Persians, and Europeans to grow politically and economically stronger. China self-imposed this isolation because it feared foreign influence after being under Mongol control and because it was ethnocentric and found little value in foreign goods. This attitude, along with the decrease in technological development (Chinese Confucianism, still prominent, favored government stability over technological innovation), greatly reduced China's previous enthusiastic trade participation and allowed a rising Europe to dominate the world in an age of colonization. Still, China remained consistently important to global trade, greatly due to the desire for Chinese luxury goods. Europeans extracted silver (the new global commodity) from the Americas and used it to pay for Chinese products. Japan paid China with silver as well. While the Chinese were exporting porcelain, silk, and spices as before, they did not import many products but rather used silver as their currency. The Chinese consumption of silver (which eventually led to severe dependency-based economic problems) kept them an active member of global trade, for they were too great and influential a country to ever completely detach. However, China lost its desire to steer the world economy and in doing so handed the reins over to Europe.

China was always important to global trade during the years 600 to 1750, though its dominance and desire to incorporate foreign ideas and products decreased. These years in history are best defined by the establishment of a truly global economy, especially with the inclusion of the Americas. China's regression in trade impacted not only its society but also European society. China closed the door to the Western world (though remained connected) and allowed Europe to become the most influential and powerful area in the global economy and the world.

CHAPTER 4

Revolutions and Industry (1750 to 1900 CE)

❯❯ A THUMBNAIL VIEW

- Industrialization led the world to become truly interdependent. Industrialized nations in search of raw materials and new markets often colonized areas to protect their economic interests.

- New technologies quickened the pace of life. Populations grew and many people migrated to cities in search of work in factories. Free-wage laborers were more desirable in this new market-driven economy than forced labor. As a result, slaves and serfs were emancipated.

- Women gained some economic opportunities in the factories but were paid considerably less than their male counterparts. New economic opportunities and Enlightenment ideals pushed women to fight for political rights, as well.

- The working class emerged as a force for change. Through organization into unions, these workers were able to advocate for improving their dangerous and oppressive working conditions.

- Western culture strongly influenced many Asian and African areas through colonization. At the same time, Asian and African culture and art strongly influenced European intellectuals and artists. Enlightenment ideals such as equality, freedom of speech, and freedom of religion became very influential in many parts of the world, while elsewhere traditional religious organization maintained power and influence.

- The ideas of the Enlightenment, which said that the government was responsible to its people, inspired revolutions and independence movements and pushed some governments to experiment with democratic values. This democracy, however, extended to a limited class of people. "The nation" and nationalism became the new concepts of identity in the 19th century and would soon spread to many parts of the world.

❯❯ UPRISINGS AND FREEDOM GROUPS

North America

From 1756 to 1763, France and Great Britain fought what is known as the Seven Years' War. While the war broke out in Europe, it quickly spread to North America, where the French and their Native American allies fought the British and their colonist allies, and to India, where both enlisted the help of Indian allies. The war proved to be a disaster for the French, who lost in all three places, losing their Canadian territories in North America and their trading region in India. Because it was fought on three continents, the Seven Years' War can be called the first global war. Britain's empire in America seemed secure after its victory over France in 1763, but the cost of the war had been high. Dealing with this debt started a chain of events that led to deteriorating relations between the crown in London and its subjects in North America.

The American colonists argued that they should not have to pay England's war debt as is evidenced by the famous quote, "No taxation without representation." In 1774, the Continental Congress organized and coordinated colonial resistance, and in 1775, British troops and American militia clashed at Lexington, Massachusetts. On July 4, 1776, the **Declaration of Independence**—inspired by Enlightenment ideas—justified independence. It listed a long list of abuses by the British king amid a declaration that **all men were created equal.** Though the British enjoyed many advantages such as a strong government, navy, and army, as well as American loyalists, the war was fought from a great distance, and the colonists had the support of other European states, including France.

By 1781, the British surrendered to George Washington, and in 1783, the Peace of Paris treaties formally recognized American independence. The colonies created a federal republic with 13 states and a written constitution that guaranteed freedom of speech and religion.

France

Unlike the Americans, who wanted the right to self-govern, revolutionaries in France wanted to replace the "old order" with completely new political, social, and cultural structures. The causes of their discontent included large war debts, a large tax burden on the peasants, and an increasing gap between the rich and poor. The king was forced to call a meeting of the Estates-General (a legislative body) in hopes of addressing the war debts by increasing taxes on the nobility. The three estates consisted of the Roman Catholic clergy (less than 1 percent of the population), the nobility (2 percent), and the peasants (about 98 percent).

The Third Estate was further differentiated by three subdivisions. **Peasants and serfs** made up the bulk of the Third Estate but had no voice in government and still lived under feudal conditions, including extensive taxation and labor service to the nobles. The **townsfolk**, workers in the cities, earned wages and were mostly concerned with getting enough bread to feed their families. Finally, the merchants, bankers, and other businessmen made up a class called the **bourgeoisie**. The bourgeoisie were the leaders of the Third Estate.

After the revolutionaries succeeded in overthrowing the French monarchy, the revolution took a radical turn. The Committee for Public Safety, led by Maximilien Robespierre, took over the government of France and instigated a "Reign of Terror," executing many aristocrats. Eventually, the revolution turned on the very radicals who had started it, and it thrust France into war with the powers of Europe. The kingdoms of Austria, Britain, and Russia formed a coalition to defeat France and undo the revolution. The creation of a large revolutionary army to defend France helped catapult **Napoleon Bonaparte** to power. He named himself First Consul, then Consul for Life, and finally Emperor. In 1804, Napoleon issued his moderate Civil Code, which affirmed the political and legal equality of all adult men, established a merit-based society, and protected private property. However, it also limited free speech and allowed censorship of the newspapers. Napoleon and his army defeated many of the powers of Europe and took control of much of the continent. The Napoleonic era lasted from 1804 to 1815, as warfare ranged from Europe to North Africa and the Middle East. Taking on Russia in 1812 proved fatal, however, as the army did not survive the winter campaign. Following Napoleon's defeat by the British at Waterloo, the powers of Europe met at the **Congress of Vienna** in 1815 to restore the French monarchy and protect the old regimes. Attempted revolutions (most notably in 1830 and 1848) continued to shake the old monarchies throughout the 1800s.

Haiti

The island of Hispaniola in the Caribbean was a major center of **sugar production.** The Spanish controlled the east (**Santo Domingo**) and the French controlled the west (**Saint Domingue**), one of the richest of all the European colonies. Saint Domingue's population consisted of 40,000 white French settlers, 30,000 **gens de couleur** (free people of color), and 500,000 black slaves, most born in Africa. There was also a large community of escaped slaves, known as **maroons**. The French colonial government had sent 800 gens de couleur to fight in the American Revolution, and they returned with ideas of reforming their own society. When the French Revolution broke out in 1789, the white settlers sought the right to govern themselves but opposed extending political and legal equality to the gens de couleur. This led to civil war between these two groups.

While these two groups were in conflict, a **slave revolt** occurred in August of 1791. As a result, the whites, gens de couleurs, and enslaved Africans battled each other. French troops—and later, British and Spanish troops—invaded the island in hopes of gaining control. The slaves, however, were led by Toussaint Louverture, who built a strong and disciplined army that, by 1797, controlled most of Saint Domingue. In 1801, a constitution was written that granted equality and citizenship to all, and in 1803, independence was declared. By 1804, Haiti was the **second independent republic in the western hemisphere,** and it was the first republic that abolished slavery. Great economic difficulty followed independence, however. Many nations such as the United States refused to recognize or conduct trade with Haiti because of slave emancipation, and small farmers were not as productive as the former large-scale plantations.

Latin America

In Latin America, the colonies controlled by the Spanish and Portuguese were comprised of a governing class of 30,000 *peninsulares*; 3.5 million Creoles; and 10 million in less-privileged classes including black slaves, indigenous people, and those of mixed racial backgrounds. The Creoles were wealthy from the plantation economy and trade, but they had grievances about the administrative control and economic regulations of the colonies. They did not seek social reform but rather sought to displace the powerful *peninsulares*. Napoleon's invasion of Spain and Portugal in 1807 weakened the authority of those countries in the colonies, and by 1810, revolts were occurring in Argentina, Venezuela, and Mexico. In Mexico, a peasant rebellion was led by Father Miguel de Hidalgo, but conservative Creole forces gained control of the movement. The Creole Simon Bolivar led the revolts in South America and by 1824 deposed the Spanish armies. His goal was to achieve a United States of Latin America, but unity did not last.

In Brazil, the Portuguese royal family had fled there when Napoleon invaded in 1807. When the king returned in 1821 he left his son, Pedro, to rule as regent. Pedro agreed to the demands of the Creoles and declared Brazil independent. As a result of these independence movements, the Creoles became the dominant class, and many of the *peninsulares* returned to Europe. Society remained quite stratified, and slavery continued. The wealth and power of the Roman Catholic Church remained, and the lower classes continued to be repressed.

❯❯ PATRIOTISM AND THE NATION-STATE

Britain had made itself the model of an imperial power with a strong military and commercial base. Older powers—such as Russia and Austria—showed their age as their autocratic traditions created increasing tension within their large empires. During the 19th century, people came to identify as part of a community called a **nation.** The forces that drew these people together were a common language, customs, cultural traditions, values, historical experiences, and sometimes religion.

Unification of Italy and Germany

The spirit of nationalism was rising in two regions. On the Italian peninsula, the Roman Catholic Church still had great influence and discouraged the growth of Italian nationalism. Under the leadership of **Garibaldi** in the south, young men pushed for an Italian nation, fighting a military campaign to unite the people behind this idea. In the north, **Count Camillo di Cavour,** the prime minister to King Emmanuel II of Sardinia, aligned with France and expelled Austria from northern Italy. Finally, a power struggle between these two nationalist leaders was resolved in 1870, the nation of Italy was proclaimed, and the king of Sardinia was chosen as its sovereign.

Farther north, the kingdom of **Prussia** was becoming more powerful after the defeat of Napoleon. The chancellor of Prussia, **Otto von Bismarck,** had a vision of a united Germany and so engineered a series of wars with Denmark and Austria to consolidate territory. The final stroke was to maneuver France into declaring war on Prussia and to use that as a pretext for gathering all the German domains together to fight as one. The war was a resounding victory for Prussia, and Bismarck proclaimed the birth of the German nation. France was in decline, and Germany would now begin to rival Great Britain as an industrial producer and leader in technology.

Zionism

One problem with the formation of nations was the issue of **minority** populations. Often, a minority living within a nation did not fit the nation's identity. One such group was the Jews. The Jews did not have their own territory but rather lived as a minority in other nations. As **anti-Semitism** (hostility or prejudice toward Jews or Judaism) rose in the 19th century, so did the Zionist movement. This movement sought to establish a Jewish state in Palestine. A Jewish reporter, Theodor Herzl, launched the Zionist movement in 1897.

Latin America

By the 1830s, most of Latin America was made up of independent nations. The leaders of these independence movements had hoped to create representative governments with freedom of commerce and protection of private property. **Early constitutions** were written to create order and representation, but voting restrictions regarding property and literacy were instituted. Some early leaders, like **Simon Bolivar**, dreamed of a unified nation, but regional rivalries and economic competition prevented that from occurring.

These new nations faced many problems, such as economies that had been disrupted by many years of warfare and large armies that were loyal to regional commanders (**caudillos**) instead of the new national government. Most leaders agreed that the governments should be republics but disagreed on what kind—a strong central government or a regional state-based government. Additionally, the role of the **Catholic Church** remained strong. Few questioned its doctrines, but many wanted to limit its role in civil life. In Mexico, for example, politics was a struggle between conservatives and liberals, and instability and financial difficulty made it a target for **foreign intervention** by the United States and Europe.

❯ INDUSTRIALIZATION

The rise of modern industry was a direct outcome of the scientific activity and inventions of the 1600s. Water power was being harnessed to create mechanical energy, which would run more efficient mills. A machine that pumped water out of mines was patented in 1769. It ran

Factors of Industrialization

- Technical knowledge and invention
- A large population to serve as a workforce
- Possession of natural resources like coal and iron ore
- Investment capital (money) to build factories
- A stable and capitalist-minded government

on coal that heated water, and the steam pressure was used to push a piston. The **steam engine** would be the foundation of a new mechanical age in which cars, trains, boats, and factories would all be piston driven. The consequences of this revolution would impact human labor, consumption, family structure, and much more.

Changes in Industry

Before Industrialization	After Industrialization
• Agricultural/rural economy	• Manufacturing/urban economy
• Family-farm economy	• Wage-earning economy
• Home-based manufacturing	• Factory-based manufacturing
• Rural population	• Urban population

Preconditions for Industrialization

Several factors encouraged industrialization, including resources and technology, and England possessed all of them in the early 1700s, making it the first country to leap into the industrialization arena. Poorer nations often have plenty of people, but they struggle to come up with investment capital and a stable government to help industrialization. France and the United States were close behind Great Britain in developing industrial capability. The United States and Germany both surpassed Britain in terms of steel production by 1900, while other nations such as Russia lagged behind.

Technology

Major developments in technology took place prior to 1914. Higher-grade steel was adapted for use in transportation and weaponry. Naval warships transitioned from wind-powered wooden frigates to engine-driven steel ships weighing many tons. Trains revolutionized transportation for industrialized nations and were transplanted to their Asian and African colonies.

Impact on Gender, Family, and Social Structures

Industrialization greatly impacted gender roles and families and radically altered traditional social structures. Slavery declined, because slaves could not pay for industrial products as did free-wage laborers. The family, which had been an economic unit, moved that economic production outside the home. Working-class women and children entered the workforce as low paid factory laborers. Men's status increased because industrial work and earning wages were considered more important than domestic work. Middle-class values became distinct from those of the working class. Middle-class women generally did not work outside the home but instead were pressured to conform to a new model of behavior often referred to as the **"cult of domesticity."**

Global Effects of Industrialization

As a result of industrialization, a new **global division of labor** emerged. Industrial societies needed raw materials from distant lands, and demand grew for materials such as raw cotton from India and Egypt and rubber from Brazil and the Congo. Latin America, sub-Saharan Africa, South Asia, and Southeast Asia became dependent on exporting cash crop products to industrialized nations but established little or no industrialization themselves. Most of the profits from these cash crops went abroad, and wealth was concentrated in the hands of few. The **dependency theory** attempts to explain the uneven result of development. Instead of underdevelopment being a result of failed modernization, it claims that underdevelopment and development are part of the same process because the development of some areas is achieved at the expense of others. One example of this would be the development of a cash crop economy in Africa, which reinforced Africans' dependency on European manufactured goods.

REACTIONS TO INDUSTRIALIZATION

SOCIALISM

As the 19th century progressed, the ideas of tolerance and egalitarianism from the Enlightenment inspired many political movements. Some were revolutionary, while others were liberal or reformist. As the Industrial Revolution redefined both society and the economy, other tensions arose. The appalling conditions that workers experienced in the 1800s inspired **anticapitalist reform** and revolutionary movements. Under the broad title of **socialism**, these movements critiqued the money economy and suggested instead a utopian alternative—an economy that was run by the workers. The utopians sought to create self-sufficient communities in which property was owned in common and work was shared. One of the most prominent socialist thinkers was **Karl Marx,** who advocated the **overthrow of the moneyed classes** and the establishment of a "workers' state." Socialist movements ranged from revolutionary to liberal.

UNIONISM

Less radical was the union movement, which advocated the organization of workers so that they could negotiate with their employers for better wages and working conditions. Unionization led to extreme tensions and considerable bloodshed: factories fought to stop workers from banding together, and workers fought to remain unified. As a left-wing movement, unionism was often accused of being socialistic. The lines became blurred, as some workers became radicalized and adopted violence as a tactic.

❯❯ POLITICAL REFORM AND RESPONSES

Ottoman Empire

By the 1700s, the armies of the Ottoman Empire had fallen behind those of Europe in both strength and technology. The central government was becoming less effective, while the provinces were becoming increasingly independent—often controlling their own private armies.

In 1800, Egypt was a semi-independent province of the Ottoman empire that was ruled by **Muhammad Ali,** who was appointed governor in 1805. He built a powerful army and sponsored industrialization in the areas of cotton textiles and armaments. Egypt remained nominally subordinate to the sultan, but by 1820, Ali was the effective ruler of Egypt. His son went on to commission a French firm to build the **Suez Canal,** which opened in 1869. This transformed Egypt into a crucially strategic location, home of a link between Europe and its empires in Asia and East Africa. In addition to losing territory, the Ottomans also experienced a decrease in trade. They were circumvented as Europe began to trade directly with India and China. Also, much trade shifted to the Atlantic Ocean, in which the Ottomans had no involvement. European products flowed into the empire, and it began to depend heavily on foreign loans. Europeans were even given **capitulations** (special rights and privileges), such as being subject to only their own laws, not those of the Ottomans. All of this was a great blow to the empire's ego.

The empire did attempt to reform itself beginning with the rule of **Mahmud II** (1803–1809). Mahmud organized a more effective army and a system of secondary education, and he built new roads, telegraph lines, and a postal service. These reforms continued into the **Tanzimat Era** (1839–1876), when the government used the French legal system as a guide to reform its own laws. Additionally, public trials and equality before the law were instituted for Muslims and those from other religious groups. These reforms were met with much opposition, particularly from religious conservatives and the Ottoman bureaucracy. The **Young Turks,** a group of exiled Ottoman subjects, pushed for universal suffrage, equality before the law, and the emancipation of women. In 1908, they led a coup that overthrew the sultan and set up a "puppet" sultan whom they controlled. Though the Ottoman Empire had attempted to reform and change with the times, it was weak and vulnerable by the end of the 19th century.

Russia

Much like the Ottoman Empire, the Russian Empire was autocratic, multiethnic, multilingual, and multicultural. The ruling czars were supported by both the Russian Orthodox Church and the noble class, which owned most of the land. The peasants were the majority of the population, and the institution of serfdom guaranteed social stability. But unlike the Ottomans, who were losing territory, the Russian Empire had **vastly expanded**—east to Manchuria, south into the Caucasus and Central Asia, and southwest to the Mediterranean. Its military power and strength was not up to par with that of Europe, however, as demonstrated by its defeat in the **Crimean War** (1853–1856). The Crimean War highlighted the weakness of Russia's military and economy as compared to Europe's, pushing the government to modernize. A first step was the **emancipation of the serfs** by Czar Alexander II in 1861. He also created district assemblies (**zemstvos**) in 1864, where all classes had elected representatives but were subordinate to czarist authority.

Policies designed to stimulate economic development were issued, such as the construction of the **Trans-Siberian Railroad** (1891–1913) and the remodeling of the state bank. This relatively fast-paced, government-sponsored industrialization led to many peasant rebellions and industrial worker strikes. The government limited the maximum workday to 11.5 hours in 1897 as a response, though it also prohibited trade unions and outlawed strikes. Anti-government protest increased through the involvement of university students and intellectuals known as the **intelligentsia.** The more these groups were repressed by the government, the more radical they became. A member of the Land and Freedom Party assassinated Czar Alexander II in 1881, bringing an end to government reform. The new czars used repression—not reform—to control the people. Czar Nicholas II, in an attempt to deflect attention from the growing opposition, focused on expansion through the **Russo–Japanese War** in 1904, but the Russians suffered a defeat.

In January 1905, a group of workers marched to the czar's Winter Palace to petition and were killed by government troops. The **Bloody Sunday** massacre set off anger and rebellion across the empire; as a whole this conflict was known as the Revolution of 1905. The government made concessions by creating a legislative body called the Duma, but in reality, not much changed in Russia.

China

The Qing had grown more and more ineffective as rulers of China. New food crops brought about a rapid population increase. During the Qing dynasty, it is estimated that the Chinese population quadrupled to 420 million. This increase created great strains, and famines were increasingly common. A series of wars and rebellions further weakened the dynasty in the 1800s.

Aggressive British traders began to import opium from India into China. Europeans trying to trade with China had found themselves at a disadvantage. With its vast population and resources, China was self-sufficient and, along with its superior attitude towards foreigners, required nothing that the Europeans produced. Europeans, Britain in particular, desired trade with China to acquire silks, lacquerware, and tea, which was rapidly becoming the national drink of England. British merchants paid in silver bullion for Chinese goods. The amount of bullion a nation or company had determined its wealth and its strength (**mercantilism**). This drain of silver from England led its merchants to find something the Chinese wanted other than bullion. They found it in opium, an addictive narcotic made from the poppy plant. Despite the emperor's making the opium trade illegal, British merchants smuggled it into China, where Chinese merchants were only too happy to buy it for silver, which the British merchants used to buy Chinese goods, making a profit on both ends. This reversed the silver drain from Britain to China, where the number of opium addicts was growing tremendously, causing labor problems.

A customs dispute in Guangzhou led to the first **Opium War** in 1839. This resulted in two humiliating defeats for China and a series of **unequal treaties** that gave Britain and other European nations commercial entry into China. Rebellions such as the **Taiping Rebellion** placed further stress on China. An obscure scholar named **Hong Xiuquan,** who believed he was the brother of Jesus Christ, founded an offshoot of Christianity. A social reform movement grew from this in the 1850s, which the government began to suppress. Hong established the Taiping Tianguo (Heavenly Kingdom), and his followers created an army that, after two years of fighting, controlled a large territory in central China. Internal disputes within the Taipings finally helped the Qing dynasty defeat them, but the desperate ten-year struggle exhausted the imperial treasury. The death toll is estimated to be between twenty and thirty million, making it the bloodiest civil war in human history.

Sun Yixian's Three Principles of the People

1. Nationalism: Self-determination of the Chinese people; freedom from foreign influence (pertaining to both Manchu rule and European encroachment)
2. Democracy: Self-rule with a constitutional government
3. Socialism: "The People's Livelihood," which combined a desire to modernize with a desire to institute land reform in China

With government-sponsored grants in the 1860s and 1870s, local leaders promoted military and economic reform in China using the slogan "Chinese learning at the base, Western learning for use." These leaders built modern shipyards, railroads, and weapon industries, and they founded academies for the study of science. It was a great foundation and beginning, but the **Self-Strengthening Movement** only brought about change on the surface. It also experienced resistance from the imperial government. The last major reform effort took place after China's crushing defeat in the Sino-Japanese War (1894–1895) and was known as the **Hundred Days of Reform** (1898). This ambitious movement reinterpreted Confucian thought to justify radical changes to the system, with the intent of remaking China into a powerful modern industrial society. The **Emperor Guangzu** instituted a program to change China into a constitutional monarchy, guarantee civil liberties, and encourage foreign influence. These proposed radical changes were strongly resisted by the imperial household and were unsuccessful. In 1900, the **Boxer Rebellion** sought to rid China of foreigners and foreign influence. **Empress Cixi** threw her support behind the movement. A multinational force from countries such as the United States, Russia, and Japan, however, handily defeated the Boxers and forced China to pay an indemnity for the damages.

Amidst all of these rebellions and attempts at reform, a revolutionary movement was slowly emerging in China. It was composed of young men and women who had traveled outside Asia—who had seen the new liberalism and modernization of the West and hoped to import it to China. Cells were organized in Guangzhou and overseas in Tokyo and Honolulu, where members plotted to overthrow the Qing. Under the leadership of **Sun Yixian** (Sun Yat Sen), the revolutionaries attempted many unsuccessful uprisings, but it wasn't until 1911 that the Qing were forced to abdicate. With the dynasty in considerable chaos, the **modern Republic of China** was proclaimed. Sun dreamed of a progressive and democratic China based on his **Three Principles of the People,** but China's huge population was largely undereducated and unable to feed itself.

Japan—The Meiji Restoration

Japan made the most radical reforms and changes in its response to the challenges of reform and reaction, and it emerged from this period as a world power. Even as it continued to isolate itself selectively from the rest of world, it was changing from a feudal to a commercial economy. The Japanese knew of China's humiliation at the hands of the British in the mid-1800s. After the California Gold Rush of 1849, the United States became more interested in Pacific commerce, sending a mission to conclude a trade agreement with Japan. The U.S. Navy arrived in Edo (Tokyo) Bay in 1853 with a modern fleet of armed steamships. For the Japanese, who had restricted its trade from much of the world for over two centuries, this was an awe-inspiring sight. They told the Americans to leave, but this caused tense debate within the shogunate and the samurai class. Two clans in the south—Satsuma and Choshu—supported a new policy to **"revere the emperor and repel the barbarians."** This was a veiled critique of the Shogun in Edo, as they perceived his inability to ward off the Western "barbarians" as embarrassing. This was their chance to restore the emperor in Kyoto to prominence.

A younger generation of reform-minded samurai from domains distant from Edo made bold plans to undermine the Shogun. These "men of spirit" banded together to overthrow the Shogun and to advance the idea that Japan needed to modernize. They armed themselves with guns from the West, and a civil war broke out in 1866. When the antigovernment forces showed the superiority of outside technology, momentum began to shift in favor of the rebels. The overthrow of the Tokugawa regime was complete in 1868, when the victorious reformers pronounced that they had restored the emperor to his throne. They named him **"Meiji,"** or **"Enlightened One."** The nation rallied around the 16-year-old emperor, and plans were made to move the imperial "presence" to the renamed capital of Tokyo (literally "eastern capital"). This great transition in Japanese history has been called both a **revolution** and a **restoration.** Historians debate about which term to use because the Japanese did not overthrow the old order and replace it with something new. Rather, they reached into their past and used an older model to transform their nation.

The rapidity of industrialization and modernization in Japan was a marvel to the observing world. Within the first generation of the Meiji period, Japan had built a **modern infrastructure** and **military,** had defeated the Chinese and Russians in war, and had begun building an empire in the Pacific that European powers had to take note of. This was a clear sign that the industrial revolution was achievable by non-Europeans and that new power shifts were in the wind.

The Course of Imperialism

The European (and later U.S. and Japanese) drive toward imperialization had three major motives: economic, political, and cultural. Economically, the overseas colonies served as **sources of raw materials and markets for manufactured goods.** Politically, these colonies were strategic sites with harbors and supply stations for commercial ventures and naval ships. The key was to gain the advantage before one's rival did. Imperialism also stirred up feelings of nationalism at home.

Culturally, **missionaries** hoped to convert the Asian and African people to Christianity. While many missionaries served as protectors of native peoples, some saw their mission as one of bringing civilization to the "uncivilized."

Reform and Reaction in the 1800s

Ottoman Empire

- *Political*: Instituted French legal system (equality before the law, public trials) but met with considerable opposition. Empire collapsed after World War I.
- *Economic*: As trade shifted to the Atlantic Ocean, became heavily reliant on European loans.
- *Social*: Young Turks pushed for universal suffrage and emancipation of women.

Russia

- *Political*: Zemstvos (local assemblies) were created. Duma established after Revolution of 1905, but was subject to whim of czar. Czar overthrown in 1917.
- *Economic*: Government sponsored industrialization projects such as the Trans-Siberian Railroad.
- *Social*: Emancipated the serfs in 1861. Students and intelligentsia spread ideas of change in the countryside.

China

- *Political*: Hundred Days of Reform attempted to create constitutional monarchy but was halted by Empress Cixi. Rebellions like the Taiping and Boxer weakened the empire. Dynasty overthrown in 1911.
- *Economic*: After Opium War, European powers gained economic concessions under the Unequal Treaties and divided China into spheres of influence.
- *Social*: Peasant-led Taiping Rebellion attempted to create a more egalitarian society, but was eventually defeated.

Japan

- *Political*: Tokugawa Shogunate was overthrown, and the emperor was restored to power. A legislative body, the Diet, was formed.
- *Economic*: Government sponsored massive industrialization and trade. Japan rose to economic prominence.
- *Social*: The old feudal order was disrupted. Samurai class lost power, but some transitioned to roles in industrial leadership. New industrial working class developed.

INDIA

England's involvement in India began strictly as a business venture. The **British East India Company** enjoyed a monopoly on English trade with India, and it soon took advantage of the Mughal Empire's weakness. Expanding its trading posts, it began to press the British government to outright conquer and protect its interests. It enforced its rule with a small British army and Indian troops, known as **sepoys.** In 1857, the sepoys **mutinied** after they received rifles with cartridges greased in animal fat (cow fat was offensive to Hindus, and pig fat was offensive to Muslims). The sepoys killed British officers, escalating the conflict into a large-scale rebellion. By May 1858, the British government had crushed the rebellion and restored authority. It went on to impose direct imperial rule on India with a viceroy, who served as the representative of British authority. Under British rule, forests were cleared; tea, coffee, and opium began to be cultivated; and railroads, telegraphs, canals, harbors, and irrigation systems were built. English-style schools were set up for Indian elites, and Indian customs such as sati (widow burning) were suppressed. British rule in India helped to create a sense of Indian identity. The elites who had been educated in British universities were inspired by Enlightenment values and began to criticize the British colonial regime. They called for political and social reform. With British approval, the **Indian National Congress** was founded (1885) as a forum for educated Indians to communicate their views on public affairs to colonial officials. By the end of the 19th century, the Congress sought self-rule and joined forces with the **All-Indian Muslim League.** In 1909, wealthy Indians were given the right to vote, but by that time, the push for reform had become a mass movement.

AFRICA

From 1875 to 1900, almost the entire continent of Africa was carved up by European nations spurred on by the quest to exploit African resources and outmaneuver their European rivals.

In 1885, **King Leopold II of Belgium** established the Congo Free State. He called it a free-trade zone, but in reality it was his personal colony with rubber plantations supported by forced labor. The labor conditions were harsh—so harsh that they drew the attention of humanitarians who fought to end the treatment. The British gained influence in Egypt in 1882, when they occupied the area to protect their financial interests and the **Suez Canal**. As European competition heated up, the potential for conflict seemed imminent. In response to this rising tension, German Chancellor Otto von Bismarck called the **Berlin Conference** (1884). Delegates (none of which were African) were invited to establish the ground rules for the colonization of Africa; they decided that any European state could establish an African colony after notifying the others.

JAPAN

Because Japan was so greatly strengthened by government-sponsored industrialization, it too was able to enter the imperialism game. In 1876, the Japanese bought modern warships from the British and went on to defeat Korea easily. In fact, it forced Korea to sign unequal treaties, much like those to which Japan itself had been subjected earlier. The **Sino-Japanese War** (1894) was sparked by a rebellion in Korea. Japan quickly defeated the Chinese fleet, and Korea became a dependency of Japan. China also ceded Taiwan, the Pescadores Islands, and the Liaodong peninsula and was forced to sign unequal treaties. Japan then defeated Russia in the **Russo-Japanese War** (1904) over territory in Manchuria and Korea, solidifying itself as a world player.

❯❯ LEGACIES OF IMPERIALISM

Many economic and social changes occurred throughout the world as a result of imperialism. For one, many countries were transformed into suppliers of raw materials and consumers of imported goods. In India, for instance, the cultivation of cotton became solely used for export to England, and inexpensive English textiles were then imported. India, once the world's leading manufacturer of cotton, became a consumer of British textiles. **Migration** increased as well. Europeans migrated to the United States, Canada, Argentina, Australia, and South Africa in search of cheap land and better economic opportunities. These Europeans often served as a new labor force in industrializing areas. Most traveled freely, though some were **indentured servants**. Migrants from Asia and Africa, on the other hand, were most often indentured servants, and they went to tropical lands in the Americas, the Caribbean, Africa, and Oceania. With the decrease in slavery, planters still needed laborers to work on their plantations. Indentured servants were offered free passage, food, shelter, clothing, and some compensation in return for five to seven years of work. As a result, large communities from around the world migrated to new lands, bringing their culture and traditions.

The theory of **scientific racism** developed during this period. These theorists assumed that humans consisted of several distinct racial groups and that European racial groups were intellectually and morally superior. These ideas were often used as justification for the treatment of colonial peoples. In addition, **social Darwinists** adapted Darwin's evolutionary idea of "survival of the fittest" to explain the development of human societies. These ideas were used to justify European domination over their subject peoples.

Emancipation

SLAVERY

Many 19th-century liberals of the Enlightenment supported the abolition of slavery. Also, economically, slavery became **less profitable,** as protection from slave revolts required an expensive military force. As the price of sugar decreased, its profitability decreased, but the price for slaves increased. Many plantation owners shifted their investments to manufacturing, where wage labor was cheaper. Though a secret slave trade continued through much of the century, the slave trade ended first in Great Britain in 1807 and then in the United States in 1808. (Here, however, the importation of slaves ended but not the trade itself.) The emancipation of the slaves came later, though that took much longer: British colonies in 1833, French colonies in 1848, the United States in 1865, and Brazil in 1888. In many areas, however, property requirements, literacy tests, and poll taxes were imposed to prevent freed slaves from voting, and many individuals were forced to continue with low-paying jobs.

The ending of the slave trade from Africa and the eventual emancipation of slaves in the Americas led to an increase in indentured servitude to replace the slaves. Indentured servants signed a contract giving them transportation to the land where they would work, room and board, and a small wage in return for five to seven years of labor. These indentured servants came from Asian nations like India, Ceylon (now Sri Lanka), the Philippines, China, and Indonesia, which led to distinct cultural changes in many Latin American and Caribbean nations.

SERFDOM

The key to social change and reform in Russia was the emancipation of the serfs. Opposition to serfdom had been growing since the 1700s. While some opposed it on moral grounds, most saw it as an **obstacle to economic development** in Russia, as well as a source of instability and potential peasant revolt. In 1861, Czar Alexander II abolished serfdom, and the government compensated landowners for the loss of land and serfs. The serfs gained their freedom, and their labor obligations were gradually cancelled. They won very few political rights and had to pay a redemption tax for most of the land they received. Few serfs prospered, and most were desperately poor. Their emancipation led to very little increase in agricultural production, since peasants continued to use traditional methods of farming. It did, however, create a large urban labor force for the industrializing empire.

CHANGING ROLES OF WOMEN

Generally speaking, Enlightenment thinkers were fairly conservative in their view of women's roles in society. In an effort to challenge these accepted beliefs, Mary Wollstonecraft wrote *A Vindication of the Rights of Women,* which argued that women should possess the same rights granted to men (education, for one). In Britain, Canada, and the United States, a reform-minded women's movement became active in the 19th century. Women began to push for the right to vote. These powerful feminist movements sought legal and economic gains for women, along with access to professions, education, and the right to vote. In 1848, an assembly of 300 women met in **Seneca Falls, New York,** demanding political rights, equality in marriage, and employment. Some feminists, however, were wary of granting women the right to vote, fearing they were too conservative and religious and would thus vote accordingly. The movement continued, however, and Norway became the first country in Europe to grant women the right to vote (1910). Several others followed after World War I, including Great Britain (1918) and the United States (1920).

❯❯ CULTURAL SHIFTS

African and Asian Influences on European Art

During this time, European artists took note of the artistic styles of both Africa and Asia. They admired the dramatic, spare style of traditional West African sculpture, wood, and metalwork, as well as the use of color and stylized forms of design in Japan. Based on Japanese influences, the Impressionists focused on simple themes in nature, feeling that this type of art liberated them from the rules of classical painting. A new movement of modern art was soon launched, free of traditional constraints.

Cultural Policies of Meiji Japan

As Japan opened up to the industrialization of the West, it was also heavily influenced by the culture of the West. Japanese literature was affected by European models, and writers experimented with Western verse. Architects and artists created large buildings of steel with Greek columns like those seen in the West. Many Japanese also copied Western fashion and hairstyles. Amidst all of these influences, however, Japan also preserved its own values.

Leisure and Consumption

The industrial age brought higher wages and fewer work hours. These changes gave people new opportunities. The size of the middle class increased, leading to a new focus on the concept of leisure.

The field of advertising communicated to the people the sense of "needing things." The bicycle, for instance, became the "must-have item" of the 1880s. Popular newspapers, theaters, and professional sports all became popular in this new era of leisure and consumption.

The Environment

The Industrial Revolution had significant and long-lasting impacts on the environment. Air and water pollution affected the heath of urban areas; there was also an increase in noise pollution. Entire landscapes were destroyed as humans cut down forest timber for railroad ties, stripped hills and mountains for ores, and denuded areas of vegetative cover for farming. Deforestation exacerbated desertification in some areas and flooding and mudslides in others. Mechanical methods of hunting made fishing and whaling more effective with the result that many areas were significantly depleted by the early 20th century and many whale species were in danger of becoming extinct, until the discovery of petroleum products made whale oil less valuable for use as a lubricant. Improved firearms made hunting easier, often with disastrous results as animals like the bison of the North American plains were hunted almost to extinction. The invention of dynamite in 1867 opened the way to more effective removal of earth and stone, particularly for mines and tunnels. Urbanization accelerated, and the human population, about 790 million in 1750, more than doubled to over 1.5 billion by 1914. It was also during this era, however, that concern for the environment, beyond the need to conserve a nation's resources, first developed. Many nations formed forestry services, initially based on the French and then the American model. National parks and nature preserves were created to keep areas from being developed. Western curiosity and scientific observations began to note humans' impact on the interconnectedness of nature. Scientific methods in medicine and chemistry helped to find and then develop cures and preventative measures like sanitation systems, use of soaps and disinfectants, and vaccinations for many of the diseases that had plagued mankind throughout the centuries.

Practice Section

❯❯ COMPARATIVE QUESTION

Directions: You are to answer the following question: You should spend five minutes organizing or outlining your essay. Write an essay that:

- Has a relevant thesis and supports that thesis with appropriate historical evidence
- Addresses all parts of the question
- Provides ample historical evidence to substantiate thesis
- Relates comparisons to larger global context
- Discusses change over time
- Makes direct, relevant comparisons
- Analyzes relevant reasons for similarities and differences

Analyze and compare the approaches and resistance to political and economic reform in the 19th century of TWO of the following:

- *China*
- *Japan*
- *Ottoman Empire*
- *Russia*

❯❯ HOW TO APPROACH THE COMPARATIVE QUESTION

By the last essay of this exam, most students are exhausted. At best, their hands are tired. At worst, they have not managed their time well and have only a few minutes to complete a task that counts for one-sixth of their grade. As a result, the third essay is often the weakest of the group. It does not need to be this way. The comparative question (the COMP) **asks what is the same and what is different.** It requires a task familiar to historians and nonhistorians alike: analyzing similarities and differences.

Unlike the CCOT, which focuses on changes and continuities across time, the COMP focuses on similarities and differences between areas. By the time you reach the COMP, take a deep breath, stretch out your arms, and dive into it with the best that you have. Your handwriting may be messy, but fortunately AP readers are accustomed to reading all sorts of handwriting. Consequently, don't take the time to rewrite an essay to make it look more presentable—an essay cannot earn points for neatness and cannot lose points for sloppiness. Even so, try to make your essay as neat as possible: If you have sloppy handwriting, don't abbreviate words. If you are a poor speller, do not disguise the problem by writing difficult words with a few letters at the beginning and then a scribble. Moreover, don't include too many arrows that point to inserted sentences elsewhere in the essay—they just make the whole essay less readable.

Organizing Your Essay in Five Minutes

The COMP asks you to analyze a broad historical issue or issues for two areas of the world. Often several areas are listed, and you have a choice. If given a choice, pick those areas about which you know the most facts that relate to the question. Underlining and note taking are key. Even a few notes jotted down in the green booklet can make your essay more focused. You are being asked for similarities and differences between two areas in politics and economics. Not all COMP questions are this complex. Some might ask you to compare just one aspect. Yet other questions might not provide categories of comparison as this one does with politics and economics. In those cases, you will need to create your own categories of comparison. Think broadly and brainstorm about three aspects for comparison. Good categories for analysis might include economic, social, technological, cultural, intellectual, and artistic aspects.

Core Point Scoring

The COMP is scored in much the same way as the CCOT—up to 7 basic core points in five task areas. Though the essays are fundamentally different, several of the tasks are the same.

POINTS TASK

1   Has acceptable thesis.

2   Addresses all parts of the question.
    (1)   (Addresses most parts of the question.)

2   Substantiates thesis with appropriate historical evidence.
    (1)   (Partially substantiates thesis with appropriate historical evidence.)

1   Makes at least one or two relevant, direct comparisons between or among societies.

1   Analyzes at least one reason for the similarities or differences.

7   *Subtotal for all basic core points*

2   Possible number of points earned for the expanded core

9   *Total possible points for the CCOT*

Do You Go Beyond the Basic Requirements?

If your essay scores all 7 basic core points, it is eligible for up to 2 expanded core points for excellence. Essays that earn those expanded points may include some or all of the following:

- A clear and analytical thesis
- An abundance of evidence
- Comparisons related to larger global processes
- Clear mention of similarities as well as differences
- Explanations of the reasons the differences and similarities existed
- Frequent and consistent direct comparisons between areas
- Comparisons made within regions in addition to between areas. These indicators show a kind of sophistication that separates the truly great essays from the merely acceptable ones.

> **▶ AP EXPERT TIP**
>
> Make sure that the categories you pick for comparisons actually answer the question. A strong essay will have at least four comparisons: two differences and two similarities or any combination of three and one.

Final Notes on How to Write the COMP

DO:

- Treat the COMP question with the same degree of focus as the other two essays. All three essays are worth the same number of points.
- Use all of the allotted time.

- Select regions for which you have the most factual information.
- Write a thesis that addresses all aspects of the question.
- Make a checklist of tasks that must be completed.
- Include both similarities and differences between the two areas.
- Use comparative words to join ideas together.
- Write paragraphs in which both areas are discussed together.
- Mention plenty of facts for both areas.

DON'T:

- Rewrite complete essays—rarely is the extra time investment worth it.
- Favor one area to the exclusion of the other.
- Mention facts that are not focused on the topic of the question.
- Discuss each area in isolation.

❯❯ COMPARATIVE QUESTION: SAMPLE RESPONSE

During the 19th century, several nations were faced with the need to react to shifts in the industrializing world and were forced to make the necessary political reforms to deal with these changes. Russia and China both attempted to reform their countries, and both combated internal resistance to a totally modern transformation. Russia's government struggled for economic change in the form of government-sponsored industrialization, but resisted most political alterations and, instead, held onto its absolute monarchy. China had some successful attempts at reform and industrialization, but internal rebellions and imperial resistance to change prevented any significant reform from developing. Consequently, by the end of the 1800s, both dynasties were on the edge of revolution.

Economically, Russia was more triumphant at reform than China. The Russian serfs were freed in 1861 in the hopes of establishing an urban working class that would be employed in the developing industrial factories. Under the authority of finance minister Serge Witte, the government worked hard to industrialize Russia by sponsoring such projects as the Trans-Siberian Railroad. Unfortunately, Russia was very far behind the West and much of the government's push towards industrialization led to civil unrest. In China, the conquest of the British in the Opium Wars forced the Qing dynasty to sign a sequence of unequal treaties with European powers, allowing them to establish exclusive trading rights in China and dominate commerce. As a result, the factories and railroads built in China were built and controlled by foreigners, and the Chinese saw little of the profits.

Politically, both Russia and China were opposed to to long-lasting change. In Russia, the czar did free the serfs and allowed for the creation of zemstvos, or local assemblies, but any real efforts at curtailing his own power were eluded. After Czar Alexander II was assassinated, the czars who followed were even more oppressive and more unwilling to enact political change. This came to a head during Bloody Sunday in 1905, when a group visited the czar's winter palace to present a petition, but was met with gunfire instead of support. The Revolution of 1905 followed after the czar permitted the creation of a duma, or parliament, but the czar would simply veto this body's decisions if he did not approve of them. China also struggled with political change because of imperial opposition. Additionally, internal rebellions such as the Taiping Rebellion disrupted the country and highlighted the growing chaos and dissatisfaction with the Qing dynasty. The government attempted reforms during the Self-Strengthening movement, but much of these reforms were not really carried out. During the 100 Days of Reform, the emperor of China suggested the establishment of a constitutional monarchy, but he was soon deposed by the Empress

Dowager and his visions of reform were never fulfilled. In 1900, a group called the Boxers rebelled against foreign control in China. The Empress Dowager gave the group her support, hoping they could eliminate foreign influence, but the Qing dynasty was proven politically bankrupt when foreign powers had to squelch the rebellion. By 1911, the last Chinese dynasty was completely overthrown.

The 19th century presented the world with many new economic and political concerns. Those countries that successfully reformed and reacted, both politically and economically, survived and became powerful in the 20th century. Those that could not reform and react, like Russia and China, lost control of their empires politically and economically (and even culturally, to a degree), and were eventually overthrown.

CHAPTER 5

Modern Times
(1900 CE to Present)

❯❯ A THUMBNAIL VIEW

- Due to improvements in nutrition and healthcare, and the decrease of the death rate, the world population went from 1 billion people in 1900 to over 6 billion today. The movement of people has also increased throughout the world, with many in search of better economic opportunities. Some refugees, too, are being forced to leave their homelands. Though healthcare has improved tremendously, epidemic diseases such as AIDS and malaria have continued to plague the world, particularly in developing countries with the least access to new medicines.

> **❯ AP EXPERT TIP**
>
> Throughout your review of World History, try to keep in mind the helpful acronym "PERSIA" (Political, Economic, Religious, Social, Intellectual, and Arts) and look for these currents existing or emerging during various periods.

- Traditional social structures have been challenged as a result of movements that have attempted to empower the working and peasant classes, such as the introduction of communist governments in various parts of the world. As the European Union develops and becomes more interconnected and religious fundamentalism grows, are nation-states losing their political hold?

- Women gained the right to vote in many parts of the world as well as access to new economic opportunities and education. The development of the birth control pill empowered women by allowing them to control their own reproductive systems.

- The world became more and more integrated through technology, cultures blended, and some came to dominate. At the same time, religious fundamentalism has developed in some regions, possibly to combat this Western-dominated global culture. The pace and rate of interaction has grown rapidly during this period. From the world wars to the United Nations to the World Trade Organization, the world became closely connected, not always with positive results.

- The rise of the nation-state and nationalism led to the adoption of political systems from totalitarianism to democracy. At the same time, the rise of a more globally connected world may blur the lines of the nation-state. Intellectually, the developments of the 20th century boggle the mind. From the airplane to the atom bomb, discoveries in math, science, and technology have revolutionized how we live.

- The world wars demonstrated the influence of technology on warfare, but they also signaled the decline of Europe as the global power. Colonial areas asserted themselves and fought for independence, but they were later faced with a new global conflict called the Cold War. Since then, nations have made attempts at both economic and political reforms, and international and multinational organizations have attempted to form a new world order. The development of nuclear weapons changed the nature of war. During the Cold War, the major goal was to stop the other side from dominating. Now that more nations have access to weapons of mass destruction, diplomatic issues are more important than ever.

❯❯ WORLD CONFLICTS

World War I

On June 28, 1914, the heir to the Austrian throne was assassinated by a Serbian Slav nationalist. Austria accused Serbia of supporting Yugoslav (southern Slavic) nationalism and declared war. Russia sided with Serbia, while Germany pledged support for Austria. When Germany declared war on Russia, France joined Russia. Great Britain was the last major European power to commit to war, when Germany violated Belgium's neutrality on its way to attack France. In World War I, the use of machine guns and gas led to a significant increase in casualties. The war became defensive as **trenches** were built and defended. Civilians, too, were involved in the war effort, as women entered the workforce.

Long-Term Causes of WWI

- **Alliances:** The alliance system had led to many open and secret agreements between nations. Most of these were defensive plans that would protect a nation in the event it was attacked.
- **Imperialism:** Tensions stemmed from imperialism and competition for foreign colonies, as in Africa.
- **Militarism:** The arms race between the major powers—Germany and Britain, which were building increasingly large fleets—also led to a hope that military leaders would fight sooner rather than later.
- **Nationalism:** After the successful creation of Italy and Germany by 1870, other ethnic groups like the Poles, Bosnians, Czechs, and Yugoslavs hoped for nations of their own. Pan-Germanism came into direct conflict with Pan-Slavism. An eagerness to redraw the map of Europe was mounting.

THE TREATY OF VERSAILLES

After defeating Germany, Austria-Hungary, and their allies, the leading Allied powers—Italy, Great Britain, France, and the United States—were labeled the "Big Four." They called a conference at the palace of Versailles. The treaty laid down harsh terms for Germany. The map of Europe was redrawn, but Italy was not satisfied. Other nations such as Poland, Czechoslovakia, Hungary, and Yugoslavia were all created in 1919. President Woodrow Wilson entered the Versailles meetings with his plan, called the **Fourteen Points.** In it, he called for self-determination (the right of people to choose their own form of government), free trade, disarmament, fair treatment of colonial peoples, and the establishment of the **League of Nations.** The League of Nations was established in Geneva, Switzerland, in 1921.

Impact of the War on the Allies

- Though victorious, **Britain** was profoundly affected by the Great War. It had lost a significant percentage of its youth, and its economy was strained.
- **Italy** was one of the Allied leadership nations and had been promised large pieces of the Austrian Empire when the Allies won. Italy continued to press for more territory along the Adriatic coast.
- The **United States** was elevated to a world-power status but was not really interested in playing that role. Conservatives won the White House and the country largely retreated from European affairs.

Germany had lost millions of troops and was forced to pay huge reparations to the Allies. Germany lost all of its overseas empire, along with provinces on both its eastern and western borders. The Kaiser abdicated and fled Germany, leaving a political vacuum. A new government was assembled in Weimar in 1919. A weak democratic Germany with a president and chancellor was created. As for the Middle East, the Ottoman Empire collapsed in 1918. Turkey declared itself a republic and, under the leadership of **Ataturk**, followed a program of modernization. Arab nationalism rose. In exchange for their help against the Central Powers, Arabs had been promised freedom. Instead, their land was carved into French and British mandates. A center of tension was the British mandate of Palestine where Arab nationalists competed with Zionists for control of the land, land they had both been vaguely promised by the Allies.

Important Powers

Russia was in shambles as the revolution gave way to civil war after 1918. Russia was not a party to the Versailles treaty because it had withdrawn from the war. The forces of the left led by the **Bolsheviks** and the supporters of the **czar** (Whites) fought to control Russia. It took two years of bitter fighting and the deaths of perhaps a million Russians for the Reds to claim victory and declare the birth of the **Union of Soviet Socialist Republics**.

Japan had fought on the Allied side during the war and hoped to add to its empire. It did not get what it wanted at Versailles, and a postwar economic downturn led to hard times.

When Japan gained some German concessions in **China** through the treaty, there were riots in Beijing to protest. This led to a surge of nationalism in China and to a cultural and intellectual period known as the **May Fourth Movement**, which resulted in the formation of the Nationalist Party.

India fought on the side of the British in World War I and had been promised self-government after the war, but little change occurred. This led to a surge in Indian nationalism and, under the leadership of **Mohandas Gandhi**, the eventual independence of India in 1947.

Global Depression

The economy of the United States was crucial to the health of world markets. When the stock market collapsed in October 1929, American and foreign investors lost billions of dollars. The impact was especially severe in Europe, which had depended on American loans to recover from World War I. The wave of bank failures in the United States had a ripple effect in London, Berlin, and Tokyo. The bond market also shrank, and many investors were caught off guard as they tried to cover huge losses. Global unemployment rose, and the United States passed the highest tariff (a tax on imports) in its history, further hindering international trade.

The hardships of the Depression led to political instability and a rise in political extremism. Communists criticized the failings of capitalism, while fascists on the right sought to protect private enterprise. Japan, Italy, and Germany looked to dictatorial rule in an effort to pull out of economic hardship. In the 1930s in Japan, the military replaced civilian politicians. Lacking natural resources, Japan needed to procure crucial minerals for its own industrial needs. It

Causes of Global Depression

- Overdependence on American loans and buying
- Increase in tariffs and protectionism
- Industrial and farming surpluses leading to deflation
- Poor banking management

had already gained Taiwan and Korea, but it now fixed its eye on northeast China. **Japan's invasion of Manchuria** in 1931 led to protests, but the Japanese kept their new territory and soon left the League of Nations. Similarly, **Italy invaded Ethiopia** in 1935.

❯❯ RISE OF FASCIST AND TOTALITARIAN STATES

Italy

The triumph of Marxist revolution in Russia after 1921 had great impact on world political thinking in the 1920s, and fear about the spread of communism led to new political movements. It was in Italy that the first expression of anti-communism emerged. A small group of men led by the fascist **Benito Mussolini** marched on Rome in 1922, demanding that they be allowed to form a government. The king gave in to this demand, and Italy was soon dominated by Mussolini.

Fascism as an Ideology

- Opposition to communism as a threat to tradition and private property
- Ultra-nationalism and glorification of the state
- Militarism and glorification of war as the ultimate expression of power
- Alliances with big business and destruction of the labor unions
- Rejection of liberalism and democracy, which were seen as weak and ineffective

Soviet Union

Lenin, the architect of the Russian Revolution, died of a stroke seven years after the revolution. The power struggle within the Bolshevik party led to the rise of **Josef Stalin,** who took control in 1927. Stalin's ruthless elimination of all his rivals allowed him to take complete power by the 1930s. His leadership became associated with Soviet communism and is also called **Stalinism**.

Stalinism as Practiced

- Centralized control of the economy
- World leadership of the international communist movement
- Forced collectivization of all farming
- Promotion of atheism and repression of organized religion

Germany

Germany rebuilt its government as a parliamentary democracy. Burdened with war debts and inflation, the new government tried to reestablish Germany's place in the international arena. With the Depression, many feared that Germany would become the next communist state. One of the political parties was the **National Socialist German Workers' Party**

Totalitarian Regime

- A single leader with almost unquestioned authority
- A single party in charge of all government
- Creation of a police state to terrorize and control the populace
- Aggressive elimination of all opposition groups

(the **Nazi Party**). Its leader, **Adolf Hitler**, spoke out against communism and used anti-Semitic racism to suggest that communism was a global conspiracy organized by Jewish people. Hitler also preached ultra-nationalism and the promise of a greater Germany. In 1933, he was appointed chancellor through aggressive anti-communist propaganda. He became dictator, or führer, within a few years by eliminating most of his political opponents. He reorganized the government by inserting the Nazi party into many areas of national life.

The League of Nations

The Treaty of Versailles had created a **League of Nations**, an organization made up of mostly European nations but also Ethiopia, Japan, Siam, and many Latin American nations. The United States, which was conservative and isolationist after World War I, never joined. The League was never successful on a large scale with its primary purpose of stopping international conflict. The League failed to act after the Japanese invasion of Manchuria, the Italian invasion of Ethiopia, and the Spanish Civil War. This emboldened Hitler, who began his own expansion of German territory within Europe unopposed. The policy of **appeasement** culminated in the 1939 **Munich Agreement** in which Britain and France handed Hitler a largely German-speaking population in northern Czechoslovakia. Despite its many failings, the League had some successes, notably with combating malaria in Europe, stopping labor abuses, limiting the distribution of opium products, and further stopping the slave trade in Africa and Asia.

The Spanish Civil War

In the 1930s, Spain was barely industrialized, with a growing urban population and a largely semifeudalistic countryside controlled by the rich and the Roman Catholic Church. In 1932, the king abdicated, and a republic was created. The first republican government was very liberal and attempted to introduce many reforms such as universal, nonreligious education, equality for women, and land reforms. After an even more liberal government was elected in 1936, officers in the army, led by **General Francisco Franco**, revolted and began a civil war that lasted for four years. Franco defeated the Republican forces in 1939 and ruled as a fascist until his death in 1975.

World War II

As in the years before 1914, there were tense matchups between nations, which would eventually lead to war breaking out. Historians debate when the Second World War began. While many point to the **German invasion of Poland in 1939,** the war in Asia had been going on since the Japanese **invasion of China in 1937**. Events in Europe affected the Asian conflict, especially when Germany overran France in 1940. This allowed Japan to take French Indochina, which had rubber and tin that the Japanese wanted for their military machine.

From 1938 to 1942, the territorial expansionism of both Japan and Germany was impressive. The Germans first succeeded in taking control of most of Eastern and Northern Europe with few casualties. The **Royal Air Force** managed to defend England, and Hitler turned his attention to the Soviet Union. In 1941, Germany launched a surprise invasion against the USSR, and Japan attacked the U.S. Navy in Hawaii. By mid-1942, Japan controlled most of the western Pacific Ocean from New Guinea to the Aleutians, and Germany controlled most of Europe and parts of North Africa. But the Germans were turned back at Stalingrad, and the Japanese lost a large naval battle near Midway Island in June of 1942. From that point on, the industrial capacities of the United States and the USSR were able to outproduce the Axis powers.

Millions were killed in both Asia and Europe, as camps were set up to murder political enemies. China and Poland were the scenes of slaughter, and the death toll in Europe alone is estimated at 20 million; communists, labor leaders, Jews, homosexuals, the mentally disabled, and Gypsies were killed. Six million of Europe's 9.5 million Jews were killed in the Nazis' **Holocaust.** Millions of Chinese were also killed as the Japanese pushed across Asia.

The Germans and British developed **radar** to detect each other's planes. **Sonar** was invented to locate unseen submarines. Rockets were used in war for the first time—most notably by the Germans as they delivered explosives to Britain. The most powerful weapon was the **nuclear bomb** that America used against the Japanese. Two bombs were dropped, on **Hiroshima** and **Nagasaki**, killing over 150,000 people and forcing the surrender of Japan in August 1945.

Civilians in War

World War II saw the first deliberate targeting of civilians as a strategy to defeat the opposing side. From the Spanish Civil War to the Japanese **"Rape of Nanjing"** to the Nazi Holocaust to Allied firebombing of first German and then Japanese cities, civilians became direct targets in the war. This culminated in the dropping of both atomic bombs to end the war in the Pacific. New types of media (radio and cinema) propagandized the war. Terrorism, the deliberate use of violence for political purposes designed to influence a population's attitude, became a new tool in war.

Much of the responsibility for settling postwar problems fell on the newly created **United Nations** (UN). Led by the five Allied victors of the war (United States, USSR, Great Britain, France, and the Republic of China), the UN established relief agencies and peacekeeping. The United States took on many of the costs of postwar rehabilitation. The UN is a confederation that nations join voluntarily. The **General Assembly** is a forum for discussing world problems. It cannot pass laws but can suggest resolutions. The UN has three responses to military aggression:

1. Diplomatic protest and pressure brought to bear on the belligerent nation

2. Economic sanctions used to pressure the aggressor nation

3. Collective military action by member states to defend the nation(s) being attacked

Outcomes of WWII

- World War II only had two "winners" since many of the Allied powers were devastated (especially France and China). Britain was crippled economically and was already losing control of parts of its empire. Possession of the A-bomb meant that the United States was now alone at the pinnacle of power, and except for the attack on Pearl Harbor in 1941, none of its territory was damaged.
- The Soviet Union had faced annihilation and survived to emerge as a great military power. Its losses had been almost 27 million people, and whole tracts of land had been decimated. Once victorious, the USSR participated in the founding of the United Nations and in the War Crimes Tribunal.

The Cold War (1945–1989)

The United States and the USSR, allies during the war, soon developed an ideological and territorial rivalry that would dominate world affairs for over 40 years. The Soviet Union sought to control the nations on its western frontier, partly as a promoter of communism but also to create a buffer to protect itself from future invasions. The United States protested, as this was in violation of wartime agreements. Eventually, a de facto division took place, which divided Europe into a **capitalist West** and a **communist East**. In the middle of it all stood the divided former capital of Germany. Postwar Berlin had British, Russian, French, and American troops stationed in close proximity to one another. War almost erupted in 1948 when the Russians sealed off the city, denying the others access, but they finally relented.

The following year, the USSR exploded its own nuclear device, and the rivalry with the United States turned into outright animosity and competition. By the mid-1950s, relations between the Soviet Union and the **People's Republic of China** had cooled. The United States took advantage of the Sino–Soviet split and normalized relations with China in the 1970s. The Cold War took on more of a tri-polar feel, as China had its own nuclear weapons and space program by the 1970s. It all came to an end when the Soviet Union collapsed in 1991.

> **Competition between the United States and USSR**
>
> • **Technological:** The race to build bigger and more destructive weaponry intensified after the USSR tested its first nuclear bomb in 1949. The thermonuclear bomb (H-bomb) followed in the 1950s. Space technology created new competition when the USSR launched the first satellite in 1957. After this, there was a "space race" and then a "moon race," with both nations hoping to be the first. Landing on the moon by the United States in 1969 and Soviet space stations of the 1970s were some of the by-products of this competition.
>
> • **Geopolitical:** Both superpowers vied for influence across the globe, especially in the developing nations of Asia and Africa. Wars in Korea, Vietnam, India, Afghanistan, and Angola were fought with weapons provided by the Americans and Soviets.

⟫ INDEPENDENCE AND NATIONALIST PROGRESSION

India

India's nationalist movement was led by the British-educated members of the **Indian National Congress**. The Government of India Act of 1919 transferred some power to the Congress, but the government cracked down on freedom of the press and assembly. Later that year, at Amritsar, a British general ordered troops to fire on a protest rally, and colonial rule lost its legitimacy. Under the leadership of **Mohandas Gandhi,** the Indian nationalist movement grew. His use of **ahimsa** (nonviolence) and **civil disobedience** against unjust laws effectively challenged British authority. Gandhi was unsuccessful, however, in allying with Muslim leadership, and a movement to create a separate Muslim state gained strength. On August 15, 1947, independence was granted to India and Pakistan (the Muslim-dominated area led by Muhammad Ali Jinnah). This division led to a mass migration of Muslim and Hindu refugees and terrible violence. Gandhi was devastated by the division of India and was later assassinated by a Hindu radical.

Sub-Saharan Africa

By 1914, almost all of Africa had been carved up by European powers. Economically, it had been transformed into a **monoculture** of cash crops and mines of precious metals such as gold and diamonds. Labor organizations, social clubs, literary circles, and youth movements all became vehicles for protest. The process of independence itself varied widely across Africa. **The Gold Coast**, later **Ghana,** was the first to achieve its independence in 1957. Led by the U.S.-educated **Kwame Nkrumah,** strikes and protests were used to remove the British from power. **Kenya** had a sizable European population that blocked independence; this led to an armed revolt and eventual independence in 1963. The Belgian government departed the **Congo** suddenly in 1959, leaving behind chaos and civil war. The political borders created by the European colonial powers led to nations that were comprised of unrelated ethnic groups who often became rivals competing for power. This led to ethnic tension in many areas of Africa, including **Rwanda,** where conflict between the majority Hutus and minority Tutsis led to a 100-day genocide, resulting in the deaths of almost 1 million Tutsis in 1994.

The **Union of South Africa** was formed in 1910 from former British colonies, but the majority black population was granted no rights. Instead, segregation laws were enacted; this system was known as **apartheid.** Under apartheid, 87 percent of the territory was designated for white citizens, and the remaining area was for black citizens. But, under the leadership of the **African National Congress (ANC),** an organized resistance was formed. International opposition against South Africa, like the United Nations economic sanctions and international boycotts, attracted global attention. Finally, in 1989, the National Party began to take apart the apartheid system. **Nelson Mandela** was released from jail after 26 years, and the ANC was legalized. In 1994, Mandela became the first freely elected president of South Africa.

Zionism and Palestinian Nationalism

Following World War I, the British held a **mandate** (a system in which a nation administers a territory on behalf of the League of Nations) in Palestine. It made conflicting promises to the Palestinian Arabs and the Jews. In the **Balfour Declaration of 1917,** the British government committed to support the creation of a homeland for Jews in Palestine, and allowed Jews to migrate to Palestine during the mandate period. The Arab Palestinians saw British rule and Jewish settlement as forms of imperial control, however. By the end of the war, the pan-Arabism movement opposed the creation of a Jewish state, and the Holocaust increased the Jewish commitment to the creation of a homeland. By 1947, the British gave up the mandate and turned the land over the United Nations, which had plans to divide the area into two states. A civil war ensued, and Jewish victories led to the creation of the Jewish state of **Israel** on May 1948. Continued fighting has plagued this region, including the **Six Day War** in 1967. The **Palestinian Liberation Organization (PLO)** was created and is dedicated to reclaiming the land and establishing a Palestinian state.

Vietnam

The French colonial rule of Southeast Asia struggled with rising nationalism. Both France and her colonies were occupied by the Axis powers during World War II. A group of Vietnamese nationalists, under the leadership of Marxist **Ho Chi Minh,** first fought the Japanese during the war and then began a guerrilla campaign against the returning French. Minh hoped that the United States would support his movement, but growing tensions between the United States and the USSR worked against him. The **French-Indochina War** lasted a gruesome nine years before defeat at **Dien Bien Phu** forced France to admit it could not keep its Asian possessions. A conference in Geneva in 1954 created four zones out of the former French Indochina: North and South Vietnam, Laos, and Cambodia. After the French departure, Vietnam became a **Cold War** sideshow: the United States gave aid to the south, while Beijing and Moscow supported the communists in the north. This evolved into a large-scale American war after 1965, as the United States tried to protect South Vietnam from communist encroachment. The costly effort failed, ending in a negotiated peace and communist victory in 1975.

❯❯ POLITICAL REBELLIONS

Russia

By 1914, Russia was far behind Western Europe economically and technologically. It lacked the capital to build its own industry, was in debt to foreign investors, and was agriculturally unproductive. Losses in the Russo–Japanese War highlighted Russia's technological backwardness. After the Revolution of 1905, the czar allowed a legislative body (the **Duma**) to be assembled, but it was often dismissed if not in agreement with the czar.

During World War I, Russian casualties numbered over 2 million, and that led to more tension throughout the country. Among other things, worker strikes began. The disorder and chaos during **March of 1917** allowed the Duma to force the czar to abdicate the throne and put a provisional government in power. The government decided to stay in the war, and food shortages, revolts, and continued strikes led to more disorder. **Vladimir Lenin,** the leader of the Bolsheviks, promised the people **"Peace, Land, Bread"**—exactly what they needed.

In November of 1917, Lenin's party seized power; in March of 1918, it signed the **Treaty of Brest-Litovsk** with Germany, ending Russia's part in the war. For the next few years, a civil war raged throughout Russia between the Reds (communists) and the Whites (Loyalists). The **Bolshevik government** took control of the land, banks, and industries and used the **Cheka,** the secret police, to keep an eye on its people. However, the aftermath of World War I and civil war included a severe drought that resulted in widespread famine, so Lenin decided to take a more moderate course of action.

The **New Economic Policy** (NEP) instituted in 1921 allowed peasants to sell their products, but the government still controlled banking, trade, and heavy industry. Lenin died in 1924, and after a power struggle, **Joseph Stalin** came to power. Stalin instituted his **Five-Year Plans** with the goal of increasing industrial and agricultural productivity. Individual farms became collectivized (those who refused collectivization were killed, numbering over 14.5 million), and agricultural productivity declined, leading to great hardship. Industrial productivity increased a few years later, however, when Western Europe and the United States were hurting from the Great Depression. The Russian people experienced tremendous oppression during Stalin's **Great Purges** of the 1930s. Thousands were tried and executed and millions were imprisoned.

China

China was on the winning side of both world wars, but few nations suffered more from World War II. Technically, the Nationalist (**Guomindang**) government had been ruling China since the **Revolution of 1911,** but in reality, the country was fragmented into warlord-dominated zones. **Sun Yixian**, the father of modern China, died in 1925 and a young army officer named **Jiang Jieshi** inherited leadership of the struggling Republic of China. After 1921, a new dynamic in the nation was exhibited by the founding of the **Chinese Communist Party** (CCP). Jiang tried to work with the communists until he turned on them in 1927, driving them underground. Communists were tracked down throughout the 1930s until they retreated to the north and reorganized. The Japanese attacks in 1931 and 1937 rallied all of China to the defense of the nation. When Japan invaded, Chinese nationalists and communists alike tried to cooperate in their fight against the Japanese, but there was little trust.

After Japan surrendered in 1945, the United States tried to encourage formation of a coalition government, but negotiations broke down and civil war resumed. For three years, the CCP and the Nationalist Guomindang (GMD) fought each other. The communists prevailed in 1949, and their leader, **Mao Zedong**, proclaimed the birth of the People's Republic of China (PRC) from Beijing as the nationalists fled to Taiwan to regroup.

Mao's Initial Changes to China

Economic:
- All businesses were nationalized.
- Land was distributed to peasants.
- Peasants were urged to pool their land and work more efficiently on cooperative farms.

Political:
- A one-party totalitarian state was established.
- Communist party became supreme.
- Government attacked crime and corruption.

Social:
- Peasants were encouraged to "speak bitterness" against landlords (10,000 landlords were killed as a result).
- Communist ideology replaced Confucian beliefs.
- Schools were opened with emphasis on political education.
- Health care workers were sent to remote areas.
- Women won equality (but had little opportunity in government and were paid less than men).
- The extended family was weakened.

In order to increase agricultural and industrial production, Mao instituted a new plan in the late 1950s. In the **Great Leap Forward**, which aimed to increase agricultural and industrial output, all life was to be collective—family houses were torn down, and commune life replaced family life. Backyard steel furnaces were set up to use scrap metal to make iron and steel. The Great Leap Forward proved to be a great failure. Initial production statistics were grossly inflated, and the backyard furnaces did not turn out iron of acceptable quality. The policies of the Great Leap Forward, combined with the bad weather of the 1950s and 1960s, led to the deaths of at least 16 million Chinese. As a result, some modifications were made to the system. Mao's second major initiative was the **Cultural Revolution** of the 1960s. In an effort to re-revolutionize China, a group of university students known as the **Red Guards** rampaged through cities, ordered the destruction of temples, and closed schools. The military was eventually needed to suppress the anarchy created by the Red Guards. The Cultural Revolution cost the country an entire generation of educated people.

The Role of Women during the Russian and Chinese Revolutions

Russia	China
• Women served in the Red Army.	• New marriage law forbade arranged marriage.
• 65% of factory workers were women.	• Women worked alongside men in factories.
• Government ordered equal pay (not enforced).	• State-run nurseries were set up to care for children.
• Maternity leave with full pay was established.	• Party leadership remained male.
• Women entered professions.	• Efforts were made to end foot binding.

Mexico

In the late 19th and beginning of the 20th centuries, Mexico was ruled by the dictatorship of **Portfino Diaz.** Under this rule, 95 percent of the people owned no land, and foreign investors owned 20–25 percent of the land. Very little changed after the independence movement of the 1830s. In 1910, the people rose up against Diaz, and a civil war ensued. Many of the leaders, who were mestizos, wanted to break the control of the Creole elite. Leaders such as **Pancho Villa** and **Emiliano Zapata** advocated land reform. Power changed hands continually throughout the civil war, as leaders were assassinated or overthrown. Eventually, conservative forces won out, and **Venustiano Carranza** became president in 1917. He convened an assembly to write the **Constitution of 1917.** The Constitution promised land reform, imposed restrictions on foreign economic control, set minimum salaries and maximum hours for workers, granted the right to unionize and strike, and placed restrictions on Church ownership of property and control over education. In 1929, the National Revolutionary Party, later named the **Party of Institutionalized Revolution (PRI)**, was organized. The PRI dominated Mexican politics for the remainder of the century, instituting land redistribution and standing up to foreign companies, while suppressing opposition. In 2000, Vicente Fox Quesada, the candidate of the National Action Party (PAN), was elected the 69th president of Mexico, ending PRI's 71-year-long control of the office.

Iran

The **Shah Muhammad Reza Pahlavi,** who ruled Iran from 1953 to 1979, was heavily influenced by the West and pushed to modernize his country. He was oppressive, using secret police to monitor his people. Opposition to the shah's rule came from three camps: **the religious ulama,** who felt that traditional religion was being suppressed; **students and intellectuals,** who felt deprived of freedom; and **farmers and urban workers,** who were hurt by inflation and unemployment.

In 1979, demonstrations led by the religious leader **Ayatollah Khomeini** forced the shah into exile. Under Khomeini's rule, the **sharia** (Islamic law) became the law of the land. Women, for instance, were required to return to traditional Islamic clothing and were also placed under legal restrictions. Some women saw this return to tradition as a stand against Western imperialism.

Cuba

From 1940 to 1944, and again from 1952 to 1959, Cuba was ruled by the dictatorship of **Fulgencio Batista,** under which a small percentage of people were very wealthy and the masses of peasants were quite poor. **Fidel Castro** organized a guerrilla movement, which initially failed but eventually captured power in 1959. Though he had promised to hold elections, Castro did not do so. At first, Castro denied that he was a communist, but when he established close ties with the USSR, the United States viewed him as a threat. In 1961, Castro announced his communist plans for Cuba: collectivized farms, centralized control of the economy, and free education and medical services. Tensions with the United States continued when a group of Cuban exiles in 1961, supported by the United States, attempted a failed invasion, known as the **Bay of Pigs.** In 1962, a standoff known as the **Cuban Missile Crisis** occurred when Soviet missiles were discovered in Cuba. The United States and the Soviet Union compromised, and a third world war was avoided. Castro resigned from office in 2008 because of health issues and was succeeded by his brother Raúl. The world is anxious to see the extent to which the younger Castro enacts reforms aimed at economic and political liberalization.

❯❯ POLITICAL TRANSFORMATION AND ECONOMIC SHIFTS

China

After Mao died in 1976, **Deng Xiaoping** came to power and instituted a new program of economic modernization. The **Four Modernizations** were the following: industry, agriculture, technology, and national defense. Foreign investment was encouraged, and thousands of students were sent abroad to study. As a result of these capitalist reforms, the economy boomed. Deng, however, was criticized for not enacting democratic reforms. Criticism of the past was acceptable, as long as it didn't directly involve criticism of Marxist ideology. In May of 1989, massive student demonstrations occurred in **Tiananmen Square.** Students called for democratic reforms but instead were met with troops and tanks sent to crush the rebellion. The early 2000s witnessed the emergence of China as a global economic power, which resulted from policies that promoted economic liberalization.

India

After independence from the British, India adopted under the leadership of Nehru a parliamentary political system based on that of Britain. The state took ownership of major industries, resources, transportation, and utilities, but local and retail businesses and farmland remained private. Unlike Gandhi, Nehru advocated industrialization. India's foreign policy was one of **nonalignment** during the polarized Cold War. Tension continued with Muslim Pakistan when war broke out over the disputed land of **Kashmir.** Nehru's daughter, **Indira Gandhi**, later became prime minister and was deeply concerned about the growing population. As a result, she adopted a policy of forced sterilization that was extremely unpopular. Also, militant Sikhs in the Punjab demanded autonomy, and Gandhi ordered the rebels attacked. She was later assassinated by her Sikh bodyguard in 1984.

Soviet Union/Russia

After the death of Stalin, **Khrushchev** came to power in 1953 and initiated a de-Stalinization movement, which criticized Stalin's faults and encouraged more freedom of expression. From 1964 to 1982, **Brezhnev** maintained power and retreated from de-Stalinization. He instead took a restrictive policy toward dissidents and free expression. During this period, industrial growth declined; the primary problem was the absence of incentives and a system of quotas. When **Gorbachev** came to power in 1985, he introduced his policy of **perestroika** (restructuring), which marked the beginning of a market economy with limited free enterprise and some private property. His policy of **glasnost** (openness) encouraged a discussion of the strengths and weaknesses of the Soviet system. The formation of other parties and two-candidate elections were also introduced. The Soviet Union, however, had major problems with its multiethnic population, and tensions rose along with the development of nationalist movements. The republics soon opted for independence, and the USSR came to an end, as did the Cold War.

In December of 1991, Gorbachev resigned and **Boris Yeltsin** came to power. As the new ruler of Russia, Yeltsin pushed for economic reform, fighting economic inequality and corruption. He attempted to address Russia's economic problems with free market reforms. Price controls were ended and privatization begun. As a result of these policies, the poverty rate skyrocketed, reaching over 40 percent by mid-1993. In December 1999, Yeltsin resigned, and the post went to the Prime Minister, Vladimir Putin. Putin then won the 2000 presidential election.

Under Putin, consumption and investment have helped the Russian economy grow for nine consecutive years, improving the standard of living. However, many reforms made during the Putin presidency have been criticized as being undemocratic. In March 2008, Dmitry Medvedev was elected President of Russia, and Putin became Prime Minister.

Eastern Europe

The Soviet Union heavily influenced its satellite states in Eastern Europe following World War II, installing communist leaders and closely monitoring their progress. In 1956, a student-led protest in Hungary expressed discontent, and the Soviet army was sent in to crush them. In 1968 in Czechoslovakia, a movement (known as the **Prague Spring**) began in the hopes of creating a form of socialism with more freedom of speech and economic freedom. This movement was short-lived, however, after Soviet troops invaded with the intention of crushing it. Throughout the communist-controlled period, Eastern Europe did experience a rise in education and an increase in the urban working class. The former "privileged class" was removed and replaced by a new privileged class—members of the Communist Party. As the USSR was declining in the 1980s, liberation movements spread throughout the area. An independent labor movement, **Solidarity** led by **Lech Walesa**, fought for change in Poland. Czechoslovakia split into the Czech Republic and Slovakia in 1994. In East Germany, mass demonstrations in the summer and fall of 1989 led to the opening of the border with West Germany, the tearing down of the **Berlin Wall**, and the eventual reunification of Germany. Now that Soviet domination was removed, Eastern European countries moved to join **NATO** (North Atlantic Treaty Organization) and the **EU** (European Union). Beginning in 1990, ethnic conflict began in Yugoslavia, and under the Serbian leadership of **Slobodan Milosevic**, a policy of ethnic cleansing in Bosnia and Kosovo was instituted. In 2000, Milosevic was ousted from power, and he was tried for war crimes at the **International War Crimes Tribunal.**

More recently, two former Soviet republics were the sites of bloodless democratic revolutions. The Rose Revolution took place in Georgia in November 2003 after widespread protests over disputed parliamentary elections. As a result of these protests, Georgian President Eduard Shevardnadze was forced to resign. The Orange Revolution was a series of protests and political events that took place in Ukraine from late 2004 to early 2005 as a result of electoral fraud and intimidation. This successful democratic revolution was marked by a series of acts of civil disobedience, sit-ins, and general strikes organized by the opposition movement. The world waits to see if these revolutions will be the final step from authoritarian to democratic rule for states that endured almost 50 years of Soviet rule.

Japan

For the five years following World War II, Japan was governed by an Allied administration, which instituted a constitution, land reforms, and an education system. The goal was to make Japan **economically strong** so it could serve as a defense against communism in East Asia. The Japanese and United States formed a defensive alliance, which allowed Japan to spend almost no money on its own defense—less than 1 percent of its gross domestic product. Japan experienced tremendous growth through the development of an **export economy,** with a large focus on technology. In recent years, however, Japan has suffered economic difficulties, with long-lasting economic stagnation that began in the 1990s and still continues today. Culturally, it has become a more individualistic society, but it retains an emphasis on strong work ethic.

❯❯ DEMOGRAPHIC AND ENVIRONMENTAL CONCERNS

The world's population has grown tremendously in the last 150 years, topping over 6 billion people just before 2000 CE. Improved life expectancy rates through the use of vaccines, sophisticated sewage systems, new medicines, and education contributed to this rise. Birth rates in the West dropped significantly, while birth rates in Asia and Africa increased dramatically. China and India both have populations over a billion, despite the one-child policy in China and birth control programs in India. Migration has increased throughout the past century, both **internally** (when people move from rural to urban areas or when they flee urban areas due to civil strife) and **externally** (when people migrate long distances across borders in search of better conditions). Factors include a lack of resources, job opportunities, and religious or ethnic persecution. One result has been rapid urbanization, creating the new challenges of slums and unemployment.

Huge population growth combined with industrialization contributes to the overuse of natural resources and a loss of animal species. Many oceanic fish species are significantly depleted to the point where governments have to prohibit commercial fishing. Plants and animals disappear with the deforestation of tropical areas for slash-and-burn agriculture and timber operations. Smog pollutes many city areas, causing lung diseases. Water pollution limits fresh water supplies, particularly in third-world nations. The increased use of petroleum and heavy metals like mercury contribute to pollution. The increased human population has also led to dramatic increases in the amount of trash produced. Nonbiodegradable and toxic trash products end up in landfills. However, **environmentalism**, a movement to protect and wisely use our natural resources, spawned in the late 19th century, is stronger than ever. Groups like **Greenpeace**, the **Sierra Club**, and the **World Wildlife Fund** work to protect the environment. The establishment of local, regional, and national parks and wildlife refuges keeps natural areas safe for future generations.

In response to the threat posed by global warming, the United Nations held a convention on climate change. This convention led to the establishment of the Kyoto Protocol, an international environmental treaty with the goal of achieving the stabilization of greenhouse gas concentrations in the atmosphere. The protocol was adopted in 1997 in Kyoto, Japan and took effect in 2005. As of 2009, 187 nations had signed and ratified the protocol; the United States was not among them.

Social Transformations

CHANGING GENDER ROLES

In 1914, there were few opportunities for women. The fight for female suffrage saw its first successes in New Zealand, Australia, and Finland. Activists in Great Britain and the United States won the right to vote around 1920. Fashion and popular culture helped create a new image of the modern woman—free from some of the constraints of traditional gender roles. Both world wars gave women more power in terms of wage earning, but the demands of the workplace and the home continue to be a challenge for women. The postwar **feminist movement** publicized the issues of childcare and equal pay for equal work in the 1970s. Politics, law, and medicine have become more open to women in the last half of the 20th century. Successful female heads of government in Israel, Great Britain, and the Philippines demonstrated that politics was no longer an all-male domain.

The sexual revolution of the '60s and '70s further defined gender roles. Key issues such as access to **birth control** were advanced, giving women more freedom. Greater earning power in the workplace also meant more independence. The institution of marriage was challenged, and some women opted to remain unattached or even to have children by themselves. Given the magnitude of these recent social changes, the impacts are still being felt and processed. In parts of the developing world, changes to gender roles have varied. Some socialist and communist groups instituted important legal reforms for women, such as the 1950 marriage law in China that grants free choice of partners. In reality, many traditional beliefs still exist in China and other areas. The large population problem in China led to the establishment of the **one-child policy,** and as a result half a million female births go unrecorded each year, showing the continued preference for a male child. Despite having powerful female heads of state such as Indira Gandhi (India) and Benazir Bhutto (Pakistan), female **literacy rates** in South Asia are still below those of men. In the 1980s, only 25 percent of the female population of India was literate.

GLOBALIZATION

The 20th century brought about new patterns of economic and political organization that transcended national borders. **OPEC**, the Organization of Petroleum Exporting Countries, organized in 1960 in an effort to raise the price of oil through cooperation. The World Trade Organization **(WTO)** formed from the General Agreement of Tariffs and Trade **(GATT)** in 1995 to promote unrestricted global trade. Regional organizations have also formed to protect more local interests. **ASEAN**, the Association of Southeast Asian Nations, formed in 1967 to accelerate economic progress and promote political stability. The **EU,** European Union, was formed from the European Community in 1993 in an effort to strengthen European economic trade relations and distance itself from the influence of the United States. **NAFTA**, the North American Free Trade Agreement, involves the United States, Canada, and Mexico working to remove trade barriers between these countries. While the early 21st century has witnessed the emergence of China as a global economic power, the last several years have been dominated by a worldwide economic recession. This crisis, which mostly resulted from over 25 years of U.S. government deregulation, began in the US housing and credit markets in late 2007 and led to the bankruptcy and instability of major American banks and other financial institutions. This financial crisis sparked a global recession, which began in the United States and is currently affecting most of the industrialized world. Finally, nongovernmental organizations **(NGOs)** such as the **Red Cross** and Greenpeace work to tackle problems that reach beyond national boundaries and governments. As the world becomes more and more connected, cultural lines seemed to have become blurred. Some refer to this as **cultural imperialism**.

The rise of the use of the English language is also an indication of a developing global culture. Transmitted through the Internet, movies, and music, the English language has spread worldwide. Yet even with the prevalence of a Western-oriented consumer culture, traditional forces remain strong. Islamic fundamentalism, for instance, is a traditional force that very much reacts against Western culture, and the two ideals often clash.

Practice Section

1. Which of the following is NOT considered a long-term cause of World War I?

   (A) The growth of nationalism
   (B) Imperialism and rivalry over foreign colonies
   (C) Competition over weapon development
   (D) Economic recession prior to 1912
   (E) The diplomatic alliance structure

2. Which of the following is NOT a principle or feature of fascism?

   (A) Obliterating unions and the labor movement
   (B) Super-nationalistic propaganda
   (C) The growth and glorification of the military
   (D) Stressing the importance of self-sacrifice on behalf of the nation-state
   (E) Collectivization of farms and factories

3. The inability of the League of Nations to maintain order and peace was mainly due to

   (A) the aggressive political control of the United States.
   (B) the dread of the spread of communism after 1917.
   (C) the pleasure-seeking attitudes of the 1920s.
   (D) irresolute leadership and lack of multilateral military decisions.
   (E) loyal relationships forged between the major world powers after 1919.

4. Free-trade organizations developed after World War II were

   (A) OPEC and NATO.
   (B) the EU and NAFTA.
   (C) APEC and the Warsaw Pact.
   (D) G-8 and UNESCO.
   (E) the OAS and Mercur.

5. One of the significant reasons for the Global Depression in 1930 was

   (A) war debt restructuring in the 1920s.
   (B) the sustained power of the stock market.
   (C) underproduction of agricultural goods.
   (D) the development of totalitarian dictatorships in Europe.
   (E) trade pressures that resulted in expensive protective tariffs.

6. India was divided into sections as it gained independence in 1947 because

   (A) the British could not decide on definite political boundaries.
   (B) Muslims had their own aspirations to establish a state in South Asia.
   (C) Gandhi maintained the proposal that India should be a partitioned country.
   (D) Jinnah was assassinated shortly after India's independence, resulting in chaos.
   (E) Sikhs in the Punjab insisted on the partitions, refusing to consolidate all of India.

7. The purpose of the World Trade Organization (WTO) is to

   (A) discuss free-trade agreements.

   (B) purchase and sell commodities.

   (C) supervise and control world trade.

   (D) report to the United Nations about labor issues throughout the world.

   (E) support protectionism.

8. Internal migration is defined as the

   (A) importation of inexpensive labor by industrialized countries.

   (B) establishment of shanty towns in rural areas.

   (C) migration of groups of people from rural to urban places.

   (D) flight of refugees for political purposes.

   (E) the upward mobility of the middle class.

9. Countries in the Balkans and Africa have both endured tragedy because

   (A) patriotism did not develop quickly enough.

   (B) political borders were drawn without consideration for ethnic or tribal cultures.

   (C) of pan-Slavic camaraderie.

   (D) of the unresponsiveness of the United Nations.

   (E) there was too much obtainable investment capital for more nonindustrialized nations.

10. Black South Africans battled against white minority rule prior to 1990 by supporting the

   (A) UN's attempts to elevate living standards.

   (B) African National Congress (ANC).

   (C) local township councils.

   (D) efforts to desegregate South Africa's universities.

   (E) banished black government in exile.

11. The most significant reason the United States expanded its military support for South Vietnam in the 1960s was that

   (A) the USSR was threatening Berlin.

   (B) the French requested support from the United States.

   (C) South Vietnam had been an Allied power during World War II.

   (D) communism appeared to be spreading in Southeast Asia.

   (E) Cuba was aiding North Vietnam with goods and guns.

12. After the Revolution of 1979, Iran became

   (A) intimately allied with the United States.

   (B) an Islamic theocracy.

   (C) a country ruled by the Sunni majority.

   (D) gradually more supportive of women's rights.

   (E) progressively more attached to its geographical neighbor Iraq.

13. Mao Zedong abandoned orthodox Marxism by gathering political support from

   (A) the urban workforce.

   (B) disappointed affiliates of the merchant class.

   (C) rural peasants.

   (D) military personnel.

   (E) industrialists fearing KMT policies.

14. Indian nationalists wished to accomplish which of the following goals as a result of aiding Great Britain during World War I?

   (A) Territorial expansion

   (B) British citizenship

   (C) The development of industrialization

   (D) Self-government

   (E) Peace between Hindus and Muslims

15. The chief objective of Zionism was to

   (A) reconstruct a homeland for Jews in Palestine.

   (B) drive the British out of India.

   (C) establish freedom for Israel.

   (D) exact revenge on the Germans.

   (E) be acknowledged as an independent nation by the United States.

16. During the Russian Revolution of 1917, Lenin and the Bolsheviks least stressed

   (A) pulling out of World War I.

   (B) reorganization of land.

   (C) elimination of religion.

   (D) redistribution of wealth.

   (E) the significance of the working class.

17. Which of the following was NOT a principle of communist China?

   (A) Weaken family relationships.

   (B) Discourage Confucian rituals.

   (C) Destroy counterrevolutionaries.

   (D) Persuade workers to strike.

   (E) Collectivize farms.

18. Which of the following resulted from both the Mexican and Iranian Revolutions?

   (A) The conflicts led to a return to religious traditions.

   (B) Civil war between opposing groups resulted.

   (C) Foreign control and authority were weakened.

   (D) A democratic constitution was created.

   (E) The former government returned to power after a period of chaos.

19. Biodiversity and global warming are both significant illustrations of

   (A) nationalist problems.

   (B) persecution of native cultures.

   (C) improved weaponry.

   (D) military dictatorships.

   (E) environmental concerns.

20. Which of the following is NOT an action Castro took following the Cuban Revolution?

   (A) Collectivize farms.

   (B) Centralize power over the economy.

   (C) Seek out an alliance with the Soviet Union.

   (D) Establish a nationwide election.

   (E) Propose free education and medical treatment.

Answers and Explanations

1. D

Struggles for empires and national rivalries between Germany and Britain were vital factors. The increase of nationalism had helped build a unified Germany after 1870. Germany sought to rival Great Britain, and its forceful military upsurge endangered the existing equilibrium of power in Europe. Imperialistic rivalries also caused pressure between Britain and France. Alliances were forged that helped to foster a false sense of security. The shooting in Sarajevo caused war between Austria and Serbia, and it drew the other nations into the war too.

2. E

Collectivization of farms is not usually important to fascists. Big business leaders often support fascist regimes because fascism promises to protect them from communism and deal with labor organizations. Fascist regimes return the favor with strict policies on workers and other benefits for business owners. One aspect of the business–regime relationship is the prohibition of all labor unions. This, in addition to military contracts, binds industry to the government. Fascism exalts the nation above all else, and individual choice is discouraged. Young men are groomed for the military, and service to the state is the desired goal for all.

3. D

Without the involvement of the United States or Russia, the League of Nations was without strong leadership. The United States did not ratify the Treaty of Versailles, nor did it join the League of Nations. It was left to Britain and France to provide guidance to the League in Geneva, but they often disagreed. The establishment of the USSR as a communist regime after 1917 was a huge shift, but even the Soviets joined the League and tried to fit into the system of European powers. Alliances before WWII were not the model of diplomacy that they had been pre-1914.

4. B

The European Union and the North American Free Trade Agreement were established to aid in the transfer of goods between nations. These trading blocs attempted to stimulate business and create consumer benefits, such as lower prices. NATO is not a trade association but rather a military alliance formed in 1949 to thwart communist expansion in Western Europe. APEC is a loose association of the countries in the Asia Pacific region; it hosts economic conferences every year. The G-8 was formed recently to allow major economic powers to share information on global issues. The OAS is an older combination of the nations in the American hemisphere and not restricted simply to trade concerns.

5. E

Trade competition among nations led to a decline in international business in the late 1920s. Many nations such as the United States established trade limits in the form of tariffs to protect domestic manufacturers. War debts were restructured in the 1920s, but these helped the nations of Europe to recover economically before the Depression. It was the overproduction of agricultural goods that hurt farmers in the 1920s. The farming industry was in economic distress years before the equity market collapsed in New York. The rise of dictators in Europe took place both before and after the onset of the Global Depression. Certainly in Germany, the Nazis were able to use the economic hard times to gain support from the middle and lower classes.

6. B

During the British years of control over India, there were many different domains. When Gandhi advised the British to leave India, he visualized a unified secular democracy. Muslims finally broke with him and requested a separate Islamic nation. The partition of British India created an independent India and a divided Pakistan in the east and west. Britain had tried to avoid partition. Gandhi campaigned against partition and protested against the need for a separate Muslim state. It was he, not Jinnah (leader of the Muslim separatist movement), who was assassinated. The Punjab was the site of some of the worst violence during partition, but this was mostly between Hindus and Muslims.

7. C

The WTO is an adjunct part of the UN system and manages global trade. It has been attacked recently for being a proponent of globalization, which some see as threatening job security and displacing workers. Free-trade agreements such as the North American Free Trade Agreement (NAFTA) are established between sovereign states, not by the WTO. The WTO is part of the public sector and it does engage in buying and selling. The International Labor Organization (ILO) reports to the UN on labor issues. The WTO is a advocate of free trade and fights against protectionist attitudes in countries around the world.

8. C

The last 200 years have seen massive shifts of people from rural farmland to urban areas, where there are more jobs. This internal migration is one of the great trends in world history since the Industrial Revolution. Migrant workers who come from other countries would be an example of external migration. Shanty towns are a form of temporary, crude housing, usually associated with urban areas. Refugees fleeing to other countries would not be an internal phenomena, regardless of the reason for their flight. The economic or social position of the middle class does not define internal migration, which describes the physical movement of groups of people from one location to another.

9. B

Taking ethnicity and tribalism into consideration is a concept that has eluded politicians throughout history. Africa was poorly segmented by the Europeans in the 1880s, and the Hapsburgs held many minorities within their empire until 1919. Nationalism did cause considerable problems in the Balkans as ethnic groups fought to establish their own countries, such as Croatia and Slovenia. Pan-Slavic solidarity did not stand the test of time, as subgroups caused the disintegration of Yugoslavia after 1990. Ethnic and tribal tensions in Africa and the Balkans predate the founding of the UN, so it cannot be blamed. While undeveloped nations could use investment capital, this is not a major reason for ethnic and tribal issues in Africa or the Balkans.

10. B

The fight for the civil rights of black Africans in South Africa was led by the African National Congress, or ANC. Its leaders were incarcerated and tortured during the white minority control of the government until 1992. Efforts by the outside world were mainly thwarted by the white minority regime in South Africa until the end of apartheid. Blacks and their townships had no political control in white South Africa. Desegregation of the universities was not a major goal of blacks during apartheid. While there were black leaders who opposed the white regime, there was no "government" in exile that agitated abroad against Pretoria, South Africa's capital.

11. D

The Domino Theory was the fear that communism would continue to expand in Asia after the revolution in China in 1949 and the partition of Vietnam in 1954. When the French left Southeast Asia in the 1950s, the United States took more of an active role in trying to stabilize the region. Cold War tensions in Berlin were not directly connected to the situation in Southeast Asia. After losing Indochina in 1954, France was in no position to ask the United States for aid, since the French Indochina War (from 1946) was funded largely by the United States. South Vietnam had not been a country during World War II, as it was established in the multilateral resolution in 1954 at Geneva.

12. B

The defeat of the shah in Iran was led by Shiite clerics, some of whom had been in exile. After the revolution, the mullahs took power and instituted Islamic rule within the nation. Iran is mostly Shiite, and women's rights were not upheld in the 1979 revolution. The 1979 Iranian revolution was largely anti-American and resulted in the taking of the United States embassy by a local mob. Iran–Iraq relations deteriorated immediately after the 1979 revolution and led to a horrific border war in 1981.

13. C

Orthodox Marxists predicted that urban workers would rebel against their capitalist masters and the world socialist revolution would begin in urban areas. Mao Zedong adapted Marxist thought to the plight of the peasants in the countryside, and they were the instruments through which he was victorious in overthrowing the Nationalists in 1949. The merchant class tended to support the Nationalists during the post–World War II revolution in China. The number of professional soldiers in China at this time was too small to constitute a real class. Industrialists were the last group that would support Mao, as they had the most to lose in a socialist regime.

14. D

Through organizations such as the Indian National Congress, Indian nationalists had been struggling for self-government and believed the British, who promised that Indian participation in the war would lead to independence. India did not, however, achieve its independence until after World War II (in 1947).

15. A

The Zionist movement was created in the 19th century with the hope of building a homeland for Jews in Palestine. This movement was furthered by the Balfour Declaration issued in 1917, giving British support to the Jewish homeland. This also allowed for increased Jewish migration to Palestine after the Holocaust and to the eventual UN recognition of the state of Israel in 1948.

16. C

Lenin's famous slogan, "Peace, Land, Bread," laid out his visualization for Russia's new political arena. *Peace* referred to the people's wish to end Russia's involvement in World War I. *Land* meant a more equitable distribution of land to the peasant and working classes. *Bread* represented an end to the starvation and economic hardships of the Russian people. Though Lenin and the Bolsheviks later took power away from the Russian Orthodox Church, this was not something they focused on in order to win the support of the Russian people.

17. D

After the communist conquest in 1949, Mao's goals were to build an egalitarian society based on control of the peasants. He did so by binding citizens to the government rather than to their families, by pointing out the outdatedness of Confucian thought, by collectivizing agriculture, and by ridding society of the "bad" elements such as those considered to be counterrevolutionary. Through all these changes, it was necessary to maintain order; therefore, the communist party would certainly not encourage any worker strikes.

18. C

In Mexico, foreign companies owned much of the land and were reaping most of the profit. After the revolution, the new government made a powerful push to lessen foreign control over the economy. In Iran, the shah's government was seen as controlled by the West; after the revolution, an Islamic theocracy ruled, attempting to abolish Western cultural, economic, and political influence from the country.

19. E

Biodiversity has become threatened in the recent past because of the destruction of natural habits for many species as well as the depletion of natural resources, like water and oil. The earth's temperature has been rising as well (called global warming), possibly due to the release of carbon from industrialized cities.

20. D

Although Castro had promised elections prior to the revolution, this was never carried out. True to a communist philosophy, however, he did collectivize farms, centralize control of the economy, and offer free education and medical services. His alliance with the Soviet Union caused much tension and conflict with the United States as well.

Glossary

General Terms

civilization This term can be a loaded issue of historical debate. Who is civilized and who is not? Strictly speaking, a civilization is settled and agricultural. Thus it is able to produce surplus food that can support an elite class. At times, however, the term has been used to separate those cultures considered advanced from those that did not "measure up," especially during the time of European imperialism.

demography The study of population dynamics. Demographics is important in the study of world history because population dynamics provide evidence of important historical trends, such as disease pandemics and migrations.

diffusion The spread of items from one place to another. In world history, the phrase *cultural diffusion* is used to describe the spread of ideas, such as religions and products.

gender Describes the social roles that men and women adopt. Different cultures at different times have vastly different notions of gender roles. Even within a given society, gender roles may differ between different social groups, such as between the elites and the peasantry.

historiography The study of the way that historians write history. In one sense, it is the history of history. A person examining historiography would look at the way that a Marxist historian would frame history differently than a person with a liberal perspective.

interregional The connections between different regions of the world. Trade connections, for example, between South Asia and East Africa are an example of interregional contacts.

migration The movement of people from one area to settle in another area. Migrations can be voluntary or forced, such as with slavery.

patriarchy A social system in which the father is the head of the family or a system in which men dominate the social structure.

periodization The division of historical time into different periods. AP World History, for example, divides the course into five periods of history. How history is divided is a matter of great debate since it, by nature, sets up different dates as the critical division points.

technology The way in which people adapt their knowledge to tools and inventions. The concept of technology is a major theme of the AP World History course.

8000 BCE to 600 CE

animism A type of religious belief that focuses on the roles of the various gods and spirits in the natural world and in human events. Animist religions are polytheistic and have been practiced in almost every part of the world.

caste system The social system of the Aryans divided people into four castes, also known as varnas. This caste system had a profound impact on the development of the Hindu religion. Each of the four main castes had specific roles to fulfill in society.

Classical Represents a period of great cultural significance in society before the modern age. In a limited form of usage, *classical* refers to the age of Athens in ancient Greece and to the time of the Roman Republic and Empire. The term *classical*, however, can also be applied to non-Mediterranean cultures, such as the Qin dynasty of China.

filial piety A form of respect shown by children to their parents. Filial piety is a crucial concept in Confucian thought and can also be seen in the respect shown to ancestors.

monotheism The religious belief in one God. Judaism, Christianity, and Islam are all monotheist religions.

Neolithic Revolution The term *Neolithic* means "new stone age." During the early years of the Neolithic period, which corresponds to the starting point of the AP World History course of 8000 BCE, humans developed agriculture and settled into fixed communities.

nomadic A way of life in which people do not have a settled home but rather move from place to place in order to support their livelihood. Pastoral nomads move in order to find places for their animals to forage; hunter-gatherer nomads seek out new areas for hunting food.

pastoral Refers to a group of people who herd domesticated animals for their livelihood. Often pastoral people are also nomadic.

polygamy A cultural practice in which one person is married to more than one spouse at a time.

polytheism Religious belief in more than one god. The ancient Greeks practiced polytheism.

Silk Road The trade routes that linked the Mediterranean area of the Roman Empire with the Chinese Qin dynasty. Silk textiles and other precious trade goods traveled across the Silk Road about 2,000 years ago. Later, the Silk Road flourished in the Mongol rule of the 1200s.

600 CE to 1450 CE

caliphate Caliphs were the political—and to a certain extent religious—successors of Muhammad. The term in Arabic means "deputy." Four noble caliphs following Muhammad were themselves succeeded by the caliphs of the Umayyad and Abbasid Empires.

Crusades Military invasions during the Middle Ages by the Christians of Western Europe with the objective of capturing the Holy Land from the Muslims. Christian crusader states were established along the eastern Mediterranean coast until later Muslim counterattacks reconquered the area. The Crusades were also responsible for increasing the cultural and economic integration of Southern Europe with the rest of the world.

Dar al-Islam A term meaning "house of Islam" in Arabic. The Dar al-Islam is the expanse of the Islamic world. In the centuries that followed the death of Muhammad, Dar al-Islam stretched from the Iberian Peninsula of Western Europe to the far islands of Southeast Asia.

feudalism A social and political system in which lords are granted landed estates by a monarch in exchange for their loyalty, especially in military matters. Feudalism existed during the Medieval period in Western Europe and in Japan during the age of the Shoguns.

Indian Ocean trade system A network of trade established between the Indian subcontinent and the Swahili trade cities of Eastern Africa. Oceangoing merchants from the Arabian Peninsula used the regular patterns of the monsoon winds to travel back and forth carrying cargoes of textiles, spices, and precious metals. The domination of the Portuguese in the Indian Ocean during the 16th century ended the previous dynamics of this trade system.

manorialism A type of economic system in which a lord has control over the labor on his self-sufficient agricultural estate. Typically serfs were bound to the land and required to work for the lord.

missionary A person who spreads his or her religious belief to others. In several of the major world religions, such as Buddhism, Christianity, and Islam, missionaries have been vital to the spread of the faith.

pandemic A widespread outbreak of disease. Disease pandemics, such as the bubonic plague of the 14th century and the smallpox pandemic in the Americas after contact with the Europeans, caused global transformations.

papacy Referring to the authority of the Roman Catholic Pope, who is seen as the spiritual successor to Saint Peter. During the medieval period, the papacy had great religious and some political power over almost all of Western Europe.

1450 to 1750 CE

absolutism A style of government that came about in Europe during the 17th century. Absolute monarchs generally ruled a highly centralized state by concentrating power in their own hands. State-run armies, religions, and economic policy often supported the absolutist state. Many historians consider Louis XIV of France the epitome of absolutism.

coercive labor Any labor system that involves force, such as various forms of slavery, serfdom, and indentured labor. Almost all civilizations relied on some form of coercive labor up to the 19th century.

Columbian Exchange The biological exchange that occurred as a result of European involvement with the Americas following Columbus's voyages. Diseases, animals, and plants were transmitted from the Old World to the New World, vastly changing both.

empire A political unit in which groups of people, often in different countries, are controlled by a single ruler. Imperial systems are by nature expansionist.

the Enlightenment An intellectual movement centered in Western Europe during the 18th century. The Enlightenment focused on rational thought, order, and logic. These concepts had widespread impact, such as on the American Revolution and the abolition of slavery.

harem Strictly defined, a harem is the place within a Muslim palace where women are housed. Harems also refer to the women, typically concubines, who are close to political rulers.

neo-Confucianism A movement to return to traditional Confucian values that occurred especially during the Song dynasty.

Protestant Reformation The religious movement for the reform of the Roman Catholic Church during the 16th century. The Reformation led to the creation of new Protestant Christian churches, which sought authority separate from the Pope.

Renaissance The period of intellectual and artistic "rebirth" that occurred first in Italy during the 14th and 15th centuries. During the Renaissance, many elite people sought inspiration in the ideals of classical times and focused on the ideas of humanism and individualism.

Scientific Revolution A major period of change in scientific thought that occurred in Europe beginning in the 16th century. The Scientific Revolution was characterized by the use of observation and experimentation using the rational tools of the scientific method.

1750 to 1900 CE

bourgeoisie The middle class in European industrial society. During the French Revolution, the social group of mostly wealthy professionals and businessmen, who helped lead the initial phases of the revolution, was known as the bourgeoisie. Karl Marx considered the bourgeoisie to be the social class most responsible for the capitalist exploitation of industrial society.

colonialism Rule by one country over another country. In colonialism, raw materials and markets of the colony are often used to enrich the colonizing country.

communism A political philosophy best expressed by the thinking of Karl Marx during the 19th century. According to communism, a violent revolution is needed in order to overthrow capitalism and create a society based on social equality.

emancipation The liberation of a group of people from the control of other people. Typically, emancipation relates to the liberation of people under a coercive labor system, such as slavery or serfdom. Emancipation may also refer to female emancipation, in which women achieve rights equal to those of men.

ideology A system of ideas or ways of thinking that guides the decisions of a group of people. Ideology generally involves issues of politics, but it also has economic, social, and cultural implications.

imperialism The process by which mostly European countries established political and economic control over other parts of the world. This started in the 16th century and reached its height in the 19th century.

Industrialism The development of a complex economic system using the factory system of production. Industrialism is one of the main characteristics of a modern society.

Marxism A system of political and economic thought developed first by Karl Marx in the mid-19th century. Marxism emphasizes class struggle as the dominant aspect of social change and historical transformation.

nationalism A political belief that people should have pride in and loyalty to their nation and/or ethnic group. Often in nationalism people see their own nation as having special aspects that separate and elevate their people in relation to people of other nations.

social Darwinism An intellectual movement that applied Charles Darwin's biological ideas of natural selection and the "survival of the fittest" to human societies. European Social Darwinists of the 19th century saw other parts of the world as weak and thus justifiably exploited.

1900 CE to the Present

apartheid A governmental policy of racial separation that arose in South Africa during the middle of the 20th century. It was dismantled in the 1990s when black South Africans gained political power.

Cold War The period of conflict between the United States and its allies on the one hand and the Soviet Union and its allies on the other. The cold war began soon after World War II and ended in the last years of the 20th century.

consumer society A society, especially in modern times, that expresses itself through the process of consumption of material goods. The globalization of corporate brands and the role of multinational corporation in countries around the world are indicators of the diffusion of the values of consumer society.

decolonization The process by which former colonies become independent. Countries in South Asia and much of Africa became independent through decolonization during the middle of the 20th century.

deforestation The elimination of vast numbers of trees by logging operations, as in Brazil and Indonesia, or by individuals for firewood and construction material, as in Haiti. Deforestation can have dramatic local environmental impacts, such as soil erosion. Widespread deforestation has been linked to broader ecological issues of a global nature.

demographic transition The shift to both lower birthrates and lower death rates, thus leading to stable population dynamics. Demographic transitions occur in countries that experience modernization and enjoy the advantages of modern medicine and lower child mortality.

developing world Parts of the world that have an economic system in which the process of industrial development is not advanced. Much of Africa, Asia, and Latin America is part of the developing world.

fascism A political system that emerged in Europe following World War II. Fascism combines ideas of extreme nationalism with authoritarian rule to oppose both liberal democracy and communism. Mussolini's Italy was the first fascist country.

feminism A social and political movement that views women as equal to men. Feminists demand equal rights and the elimination of patriarchal control.

genocide The planned, systematic killing of a group of people. The Nazi genocide of the Jews and other groups is known as the Holocaust. The 20th century also witnessed other acts of genocide, such as against the Armenians at the beginning of the century and in Rwanda at the end of the century.

globalization The process by which national boundaries become increasingly less important as a result of economic, social, and cultural interactions among parts of the world.

guerrilla warfare A style of warfare that emphasizes irregular fighting units that use surprise attacks and unconventional methods.

multinational corporation A company with operations in a variety of different countries. The late 20th century, with its rapid move toward globalization, saw a rise in influence of multinational corporations.

nonaligned nations Countries that remained neutral during the Cold War conflict between the United States and the Soviet Union. For years, India was the symbolic leader among the nonaligned nations.

Pacific Rim Those areas that surround the Pacific Ocean. The term is typically used to discuss the new economic influence of the nations of East and Southeast Asia.

popular culture Cultural issues of common identity that bind a group of people together. Film, music, and sports are all important aspects of modern popular culture. In recent years, popular culture has become increasingly globalized.

Third World Strictly speaking, *Third World* was the term used during the Cold War to describe those countries that were neither Western allies of the United States (First World) or allies of the Soviet Union (Second World). Generally, it was applied to countries of the developing world, especially in Latin America, Africa, and Asia.

urbanization The process involved in the growth of cities and the areas surrounding them. Typically, urbanization occurs as part of the processes of industrialism and modernization. People migrate from rural areas or from other countries into rapidly growing urban centers so that they can take advantage of economic opportunity.

Index